Evaluating Value-Added Models for Teacher Accountability

DANIEL F. McCAFFREY

J.R. LOCKWOOD

DANIEL M. KORETZ

LAURA S. HAMILTON

Prepared for the Carnegie Corporation

EDUCATION

The research described in this report was conducted by RAND Education for the Carnegie Corporation of New York.

Library of Congress Cataloging-in-Publication Data

Evaluating value-added models for teacher accountability / Dan McCaffrey ... [et al.].
      p. cm.
      "MG-158."
      Includes bibliographical references.
      ISBN 0-8330-3542-8 (pbk.)
      1. Educational indicators—United States. 2. Teachers—Rating of—United States—
Mathematical models. I. McCaffrey, Daniel F.

      LB2846.E88 2004
      371.14'4—dc22

                                                                  2003026262

The RAND Corporation is a nonprofit research organization providing objective analysis and effective solutions that address the challenges facing the public and private sectors around the world. RAND's publications do not necessarily reflect the opinions of its research clients and sponsors.

RAND® is a registered trademark.

Published 2003 by the RAND Corporation
1700 Main Street, P.O. Box 2138, Santa Monica, CA 90407-2138
1200 South Hayes Street, Arlington, VA 22202-5050
201 North Craig Street, Suite 202, Pittsburgh, PA 15213-1516
RAND URL: http://www.rand.org/
To order RAND documents or to obtain additional information, contact
Distribution Services: Telephone: (310) 451-7002;
Fax: (310) 451-6915; Email: order@rand.org

Preface

Value-added modeling (VAM) to estimate school and teacher effects is currently of considerable interest to researchers and policymakers. Recent reports suggest that VAM demonstrates the importance of teachers as a source of variance in student outcomes. Policymakers see VAM as a possible component of education reform through improved teacher evaluations or as part of test-based accountability. They are particularly intrigued by VAM because of the view that its complex statistical techniques can provide estimates of the effects of teachers and schools that are not distorted by the powerful effects of such noneducational factors as family background.

Although VAM holds great promise, it also raises many fundamental and complex issues. Some of these issues may appear arcane, but the reasonableness of the findings of VAM studies depends on them. If these issues are not adequately addressed, VAM is likely to misjudge the effectiveness of teachers and schools and could produce incorrect generalizations about their characteristics, thus hampering systematic efforts to improve education. Unfortunately, investigation and discussion of the issues raised by the use of VAM in education have been fragmented and limited. In addition, much of the discussion is unpublished, and the practical import of these concerns when VAM is applied to student achievement remains largely unclarified.

In this monograph, we clarify the primary questions raised by the use of VAM for measuring teacher effects, review the most important recent applications of VAM, and discuss a variety of the most important statistical and measurement issues that might affect the validity of VAM inferences. Although the document focuses on measures of teacher effectiveness, many of the points discussed here also apply to measures of school effects. The monograph should be of interest to policymakers who are considering the use of VAM for teacher evaluations or accountability. It will also be of interest to researchers who are looking to use VAM to understand teachers or looking for ways to improve VAM models.

This research was done within RAND Education and was funded by a grant from the Carnegie Corporation of New York. The statements made and views expressed are solely the responsibility of the authors.

Contents

Figures and Tables

Figures

Tables

Summary

Background and Purpose

Value-added modeling (VAM), a collection of complex statistical techniques that use multiple years of students' test score data to estimate the effects of individual schools or teachers, has recently garnered a great deal of attention among both policymakers and researchers. For example, a recent bill drafted by the General Assembly of Pennsylvania proposes using student achievement results and value-added models to evaluate and reward administrators and teachers. In this bill, VAM-based estimates of teacher and school effects would affect salaries and career ladder stages as well as contract renewal for teachers and administrators.

There are at least two reasons why VAM has attracted growing interest. One reason is that VAM holds out the promise of separating the effects of teachers and schools from the powerful effects of such noneducational factors as family background, and this isolation of the effects of teachers and schools is critical for accountability systems to work as intended. The second is that early VAM studies purport to show very large differences in effectiveness among teachers. If these differences can be substantiated and causally linked to specific characteristics of teachers, the potential for improvement of education could be great.

The application of VAM to educational achievement holds considerable promise, but it also raises many fundamental and complex issues. Unfortunately, investigation and discussion of the issues raised by the use of VAM in education have been fragmented and incomplete. Although there have been reviews of particular approaches (e.g., Bock, Wolfe, and Fisher, 1996), no reviews have carefully compared recent VAM efforts or systematically discussed the wide variety of issues they raise. Moreover, while numerous methodological concerns have been raised by VAM researchers and by critics of the approach, much of the discussion remains unpublished, and the practical import of these concerns when VAM is applied to student achievement remains largely unclarified.

This monograph is one of the products of an effort by RAND Corporation researchers to begin a systematic review and evaluation of leading approaches to VAM. It had several goals: to clarify some of the most important issues, to begin evaluating their practical impact, to spur additional work on these issues, and to help inform the debate among both researchers and policymakers about the potential of VAM. In the monograph, we clarify the primary questions raised by the use of VAM for measuring teacher effects, review the most important recent applications of VAM, and discuss a variety of important statistical and measurement issues that might affect the validity of VAM inferences. Although parts of the monograph are technical in nature, we have avoided lengthy discussions of technical issues. Several more detailed discussions of technical issues are contained in an appendix to the monograph (included as a CD-ROM on the inside back cover of this volume) and have also been published elsewhere (Lockwood, Louis, and McCaffrey, 2002; McCaffrey et al., 2003).

What We Learned

Review of the Literature

The recent literature on VAM purports to show that teachers differentially affect student learning and growth in achievement. This literature suggests that teacher effects are large, accounting for a significant portion of the variability in growth, and that they persist for at least three to four years. A relatively small number of papers—several of them not published in the peer-reviewed literature—are the source of these claims. We critically evaluated the methods used in these papers and the validity of the resulting claims. We conclude that although the papers all have shortcomings, together they provide evidence that teachers have discernable, differential effects on student achievement, and that these effects appear to persist into the future. The shortcomings of the studies make it difficult to determine the size of teacher effects, but we suspect that the magnitude of some of the effects reported in this literature are overstated.

Wright, Horn, and Sanders (WHS, 1997) conclude that teachers are the most important factor affecting student learning. In their replicated study design, they model gains in student tests score as a function of random teacher effects and a small set of student covariates including achievement. They standardize the contributions of all variables in the models using what they call a "z-score." They informally meta-analyze the results of the 30 replicated models and find that the z-score for teacher effects exceeds the standardized contribution of every other variable in 26 of 30 models. Via a simulation study, we find that the authors' standardized z-scores do not necessarily preserve the ranking of variables based on contribution to total variance in scores. In other words, while the WHS z-scores for teachers might dominate in 26 of 30 models, this does not imply that teacher effects explain more variance than all the other predictors. Furthermore, WHS provide no evidence that the estimated teacher effects and their corresponding variance components are unbiased by contributions of other inputs to education that are not accounted for in the model.

In another report, Rowan, Correnti, and Miller (RCM, 2002) find that residual classroom-level variance accounts for a significant proportion of the variability in growth in student achievement scores. The results are robust across subjects (reading or math), statistical models, and two cohorts of students from a nationwide sample of schools. Although classrooms account for meaningful portions of the variance in all models, the magnitude of the variance explained varies. While the results are impressive and strongly suggest that teacher (classroom) effects are nonzero, the authors do not provide details on missing data, the nature of the measure, or the distributions of student characteristics—so a full assessment of possible biases is impossible.

Rivkin, Hanushek, and Kain (RHK, 2000) take advantage of multiple cohorts of students, each with three years of test scores, to aggressively remove the effects on achievement of factors other than teachers. The authors find that teacher effects do exist and estimate that, as a lower bound, teachers account for about 3.2 percent of variance in achievement. In other words, a one-standard-deviation increase in teacher effectiveness is associated with about a 0.18-standard-deviation increase in scores. While their methods remove many possible confounding factors, the estimates are based on gains and differences of scores that are not on a single developmental scale. Changes in scores, therefore, do not necessarily correspond to growth in achievement—making the interpretation of results difficult. Also, the authors restricted their analyses to students who remained in the same school and completed testing for three consecutive years. Thus, the authors' findings suggest that teachers can matter for some students in some metrics, but a more generalizable interpretation of their results is impossible.

In 1996, Sanders and Rivers (SR) released a technical report purporting to show that teacher effects accumulate over time. They report that for math tests, students taught by the least effective teachers for three consecutive years would score 52 to 54 percentile points below similar students taught by the most effective teachers for three consecutive years. This dramatic finding has garnered enormous attention from researchers, policy makers and other interested parties. We evaluated the methods used by SR used via simulation and concluded that, based on scenarios that best match the numbers reported in SR and our experience with school data, the SR results would be unlikely to occur if teachers or classrooms had no effects. However, there is reason to expect a small positive bias in their estimates of the size of these effects. Thus, the SR results are consistent with the existence of persistent teacher effects but might overstate the size of such an effect.

Given the magnitude of the SR effects, the implications of their finding, and the controversy with their methodology, other authors have attempted to replicate the result with slight modifications. Rivers (1999) replicated the design with several important changes to address some of the criticisms of SR and still found persistent teacher effects. Mendro, Jordan, Gomez, Anderson, and Bembry (MJGAB, 1998) used data from students in the Dallas Independent School District to replicate the SR study. MJGAB again found large persistent teacher effects across multiple cohorts and on both mathematics and reading scores. Kain (1998) conducted an independent analysis of a subset of the MJGAB and found similar results. The MJGAB and Kain analyses control for many student characteristics, including neighborhood effects. Thus, their estimated teacher effect should be reasonably unconfounded by other sources. Even though all these studies have limitations, and MJGAB and Kain provide limited details of their studies, the consistency of findings across samples from different locations and different statistical models suggests to us that these papers together provide evidence that teacher effects do persist across years.

Modeling Longitudinal Data to Estimate Teacher Effects

Estimating the effects of teachers by modeling longitudinal data on student achievement raises a number of important statistical and psychometric issues and requires decisions about how these issues should be addressed. Estimates may vary appreciably as a result of these decisions, and the resulting uncertainty of findings should be considered when interpreting VAM estimates. In this respect, VAM analyses of teacher effects are no different from other statistical models, estimates from which are often potentially sensitive to choices about the modeling approach. However, the analyses used to estimate teacher effects are complex and challenging, and the potential sensitivity of their results to modeling choices has not been well explored. In this monograph, we discuss some of the decisions that must be made about modeling achievement data to estimate teacher effects and the possible sensitivity of estimates of teacher effects to them. We break these decisions or issues into four groups: basic issues of statistical modeling, issues involving confounders or omitted variables, issues arising from the use of achievement test scores as dependent measures, and uncertainty about estimated effects.

Basic Issues of Statistical Modeling. Analysts generally have used one of three approaches to analyzing longitudinal data to estimate teacher effects. Two of these approaches break the longitudinal analysis into a sequence of models for single-year outcomes, which makes statistically inefficient use of information for the multiple years of data but is computationally simpler than the alternative full multivariate modeling of multiple years of data. Full multivariate analysis of the data is flexible and uses correlation among multiple years of data. This approach is likely to be preferable but is computationally demanding.

Another choice in statistical modeling is the specification of teacher effects as "fixed" or "random" effects. In the past, fixed effects were used in such efforts (Murnane 1975; Hanushek, 1972); recent applications (Sanders, Saxton, and Horn, 1997; Ballou, Sanders, and Wright, 2003; Rowan, Correnti, and Miller, 2002) use random effects specification. The two methods will tend to yield similar conclusions about the variability of teachers but will provide different estimates of individual teacher effects. The differences result from different strategies for dealing with inherent sampling error of estimated effects. The fixed-effects method uses a teacher's students to estimate his or her effect. The random-effects method "shrinks" the estimate based on the given teacher's students toward the overall mean for all students. On average, shrinking the estimate has optimal statistical properties across teachers but can be sub-optimal for teachers whose effects are far from the mean. Fixed-effects estimates can be highly sensitive to sampling error because teachers tend to teach only small numbers of students.

Omitted Variables, Confounders, and Missing Data. VAM uses data collected in an observational setting (as opposed to an experimental setting). The data collected from this observational setting can be subject to a number of problems. In particular, two types of problems arising from these circumstances have the potential to distort VAM estimates of teacher effects. The first type is confounding by influences other than teachers on student learning that are incorrectly modeled or are not modeled at all—for example, a model that does not properly distinguish the effects of teachers from other effects of the school in which the teacher works. The second type is incomplete data. In the case of VAM, incompleteness frequently arises in two areas: data for individual students over time and information on the linking of students to teachers. We believe these problems are among the greatest challenges facing VAM.

Models that fail to account for differences in student populations across schools can yield biased estimates of teacher effects. This is the case even for complex multivariate models that jointly model many student outcomes. Bias can occur when students attending different schools differ in ways that are likely to affect both achievement and growth in achievement, and the context of the school (e.g., the proportion of students eligible for free and reduced price lunches) affects these outcomes. Given that student populations tend to vary among schools—and our limited empirical findings suggest that context does affect growth in some settings—omitted variables appear to be a likely source of bias in most VAM applications. Although recent work on this topic (Ballou, Sanders and Wright, 2003) suggests that in some settings including student level covariates has little effect on estimated teacher effects, this work was unable to reach the same conclusion about context effects. In our own limited example, context effects had a great impact on estimated effects. Because true teacher effects might be correlated with the characteristics of the students they teach, current VAM approaches cannot separate any existing contextual effects from these true teacher effects.

Other effects that can be difficult to disentangle from the effect of the students' current teachers are those arising from schools, districts, or prior teachers. If terms for these effects are omitted from models, they are implicitly subsumed by teacher effects, which may bias what analysts conceive as true teacher effects. Alternatively, if such effects are included in models and teachers of differential effectiveness cluster at the school or district level, part of the true teacher effects will be attributed to schools or districts. Analysts must decide which potential error is more acceptable.

Real longitudinal student achievement data will inevitably contain incomplete student achievement records. The accuracy of estimated teacher effects in the presence of incomplete records is sensitive to models for the nature of missing data and to the analytic approach. Little is currently known about the effects of missing data on VAM estimates of teacher effects. Similarly, the links between students and teachers might be incomplete, and the effects of these incomplete links on outcomes have received no investigation to date. If incomplete test score data and incomplete links between teachers and students do in fact result in bias, it could be a large problem. The factors that contribute to missing links and missing test scores are common: students are mobile, with large proportions transferring among schools every year.

Issues Arising from the Use of Achievement Tests as an Outcome. The student achievement measures that VAM uses to define and estimate teacher effects are limited in several ways. Testing is infrequent—typically only once a year—and the tests used to measure achievement cannot measure fully all topics related to achievement. In addition, the scale for measuring achievement is not predetermined by the nature of achievement but is chosen by the test developer. Changes to the timing of tests, the weight given to alternative topics, or the scaling of the test could change our conclusions about the relative achievement or growth in achievement across classes of students. These changes would change estimates of teacher effects. While our explorations suggest that some of these effects might not be large (for example, differential growth during the summer recess), the effects of other changes could have large impacts on estimated teacher effects and require further investigations.

Uncertainty About Estimated Effects. Accurate inferences about a teacher's effect require an estimate of the effect that is likely to be close to the real teacher effect. As we have discussed, a number of decisions related to both modeling and measurement contribute to possible errors and uncertainty of the estimate. Sampling error is another source of error in VAM estimates. Uncertainty must be very small to make useful inferences about some quantities of interest, such as teacher ranking, and real estimates are unlikely to have such small sampling error. However, estimates might be sufficiently precise for other inferences, such as identifying some teachers as distinct from the mean. In one small example, we estimated that about one-third of teachers had a very small probability of being equal to the average teacher, which suggests that, for some applications, sampling error in the estimates will not preclude identifying a fraction of teachers as above or below average. Our estimates were somewhat robust to the model for prior-year teachers, but we did not account for potentially formidable uncertainty in other factors, such as missing data, type of measurement, or the effects of omitted student characteristics.

What We Recommend

Using VAM to estimate individual teacher effects is a recent endeavor, and many of the possible sources of error have not been thoroughly evaluated in the literature. Our goal was to identify possible sources of error and bias and evaluate what is known at this point. We recommend that many of the possible errors we identified receive additional review in the literature. Some of the areas for future research include the following:

1. Develop databases that can support VAM estimation of teacher effect across a diverse sample of school districts or other jurisdictions.
2. Develop computational tools for fitting VAM that scale up to large databases and allow for extensions to the currently available models.
3. Link VAM teacher-effect estimates with other measures of teacher effectiveness to determine the characteristics or practices of effective teachers as a means of validating estimate effects and possibly identifying what produces effective teaching.
4. Empirically evaluate the potential sources of errors we identified to determine how these factors contribute to estimated teacher effects and to determine the conditions that exacerbate or mitigate the impact of these factors on teacher effects.

5. Estimate the prevalence of factors that contribute to the sensitivity of teacher-effect estimates by surveying school districts and by replicating VAM estimation effort across multiple locations and meta-analyzing the results.
6. Incorporate decision theory into VAM by working with policymakers to elicit decisions and costs associated with those decisions and developing estimators to minimize the losses.
7. Use research and auxiliary data to inform modeling choices.

Recommendations for the Use of VAM in Policy and Practice

The research base is currently insufficient to support the use of VAM for high-stakes decisions. We have identified numerous possible sources of error in teacher effects and any attempt to use VAM estimates for high-stakes decisions must be informed by an understanding of these potential errors. However, it is not clear that VAM estimates would be more harmful than the alternative methods currently being used for test-based accountability. At present, it is most important for policymakers, practitioners, and VAM researchers to work together, so that research is informed by the practical needs and constraints facing users of VAM and implementation of the models is informed by an understanding of what inferences and decisions the research currently supports.

Acknowledgments

This monograph benefited greatly from the assistance of many people. Tom Louis offered valuable statistical insights through his involvement early in the project. Heather Barney assisted with procuring and reviewing the literature. Throughout the project, Sheila Kirby worked closely with us, providing considerable organizational and summative support to ensure that our work appealed to the broadest possible audience. Natalie Weaver provided tireless editorial, organizational and administrative support.

Anthony Bryk of the University of Chicago, Michael Kolen of the University of Iowa, and Chris Nelson of the RAND Corporation reviewed the document with care. Their thoughtful comments and constructive criticism sharpened the presentation of our results and substantially improved the final monograph.

We thank Dan Fallon, Chair Education Division, of the Carnegie Corporation of New York, who initiated the discussion of value-added modeling that led to this project, funded the work, and provided valuable commentary during the course of the work.

The project is also indebted to the working group of experts in the educational research community who participated in the Value-Added Modeling Workshop convened by this project in October 2002. Their insightful discussions helped us immensely in further understanding both technical and policy issues relevant to value added modeling. A special thanks is owed to Carolyn Rowe and Karen Echeverri for their work on coordinating this workshop.

Finally, we thank Miriam Polon and the staff in the RAND Publications Department for their expert editing, formatting, and production of this monograph.

Despite the cooperation, support, and guidance of these individuals, any errors in this report remain our own.

CHAPTER ONE

Introduction

The use of standardized test scores to hold schools, teachers, and students accountable for performance is now the cornerstone of many education reform efforts in the United States. Accountability systems that rely on test scores (sometimes called *test-based accountability* systems) have been adopted in one form or another by almost all states over the past decade or more. The recent reauthorization of the Elementary and Secondary Education Act, the No Child Left Behind Act of 2001 (NCLB), has made test-based accountability the crux of national education policy as well.

Despite the apparently widespread agreement in the policy community that test-based accountability should be the primary mechanism of education reform, there has been considerable disagreement about how this general principle should be implemented. One approach that has gained growing popularity among state policymakers over the past dozen years or so can be called the "cohort-to-cohort gain" approach. In this approach, the performance of students is compared across successive cohorts, and educators are held accountable for improving performance from one cohort to the next. In this approach, individual students are not tracked over time; rather, one cohort of students in a given grade is compared with previous cohorts in the same grade. California's Public Schools Accountability Act of 1999 is an example of the cohort-to-cohort gain approach. Another approach holds schools accountable for the percentage of students in specific grades reaching or exceeding a specified performance level on a given assessment. With the enactment of NCLB, this approach has become national policy. NCLB specifies that states receiving federal Title I funds must hold schools accountable for making "adequate yearly progress" (AYP) by meeting increasingly higher targets for student achievement as specified by the proportion of students classified as proficient on the state's assessments, so that all students are achieving above this level in 12 years.

A fundamentally different approach to test-based accountability is to monitor the achievement growth of students as they progress through the grades and to use statistical models to estimate the contribution of teachers or schools to that growth. Because these methods attempt to estimate how much teachers or schools add to the achievement of entering students, they are generally called "value-added" methods, using a term from the economic production function literature. In the production function literature, value-added methods attempt to determine the effects of incremental inputs into education, controlling for achievement at a point in the past. Value-added is also interpreted to mean the unique contributions of the school or teacher to students' progress over the course of a year rather than the cumulative education effects or student background factors. Here we use the acronym VAM to refer to value-added models applied to students' educational achievement.[1]

Until recently, only researchers and a small number of jurisdictions used VAM. The most prominent implementation of this approach is the Tennessee Value Added Assessment System, or TVAAS (Sanders and Horn, 1998). A few additional efforts have been undertaken across the nation (e.g., Webster, Mendro, Orsak, and Weerasinghe, 1998). The implementation of VAM is challenging, requiring both extensive data that link student records over time and complex and computationally demanding statistical methods. Indeed, without substantial investments in data and statistical capabili-

---

[1] The term *value-added modeling* is often associated with complex hierarchical models such as those described in Sanders, Saxton, and Horn (1997) or Webster and Mendro (1997); however, simpler models of growth are possible. Some are discussed in Chapter Four or McCaffrey et al. (2003).

ties—either in-house or from an external consultant—VAM would be beyond the reach of most states and districts at present.

Despite the swiftly growing dominance of the cohort-to-cohort gains and adequate-yearly-progress approaches to accountability and the substantial demands of the VAM approach, VAM has recently garnered a great deal of attention among both policymakers and researchers. For example, a bill drafted by the General Assembly of Pennsylvania proposes using student achievement results to evaluate and reward administrators and teachers. Twenty-five percent of superintendents' evaluations would be based on "a running total of three (3) years of value-added State test results aggregated to the district level," and 50 percent of teachers' evaluations will be based on "a running average of three (3) years of value-added results aggregated to the teacher level for students taught by the teacher" (General Assembly of Pennsylvania, 2002). Principals' evaluations would also be based in part on value-added results aggregated to the school level. The results of these evaluations would affect salaries and career ladder stages, as well as contract renewal for teachers and administrators.

There are at least two reasons why VAM has attracted growing interest. One reason is that VAM holds the promise of separating the effects of teachers and schools from the powerful effects of such noneducational factors as family background, and this isolation of the effects of teachers and schools is critical for accountability systems to work as intended. The second is that early VAM studies purport to show large differences in effectiveness among teachers. If these differences can be substantiated and can be causally linked to specific characteristics of teachers, the potential for the improvement of education could be great.

Purposes of This Monograph

The application of VAM to educational achievement holds great promise, but it also raises many fundamental and complex issues. Although some of these issues may appear arcane, the reasonableness of the findings of VAM studies hinges on them. If these issues are not adequately addressed, VAM is likely to misjudge the effectiveness of many teachers and schools and could produce incorrect generalizations about their characteristics, thus hampering systematic efforts to improve education.

The important questions raised by VAM are diverse and include issues of both statistical modeling and measurement. Some of these are inherent in the methods themselves, whereas others stem from their relatively untried application to growth in student achievement. Three of the topics addressed later in this report illustrate the diversity of the issues raised by VAM. First, if teachers or schools are to be evaluated using VAM, an obvious question involves the amount of sampling error in the estimates and rankings of teacher and school effectiveness. The answer to this question depends on the statistical models used and the variability in the data but does not hinge on the particular characteristics of the educational systems, such as the method used for assigning students to schools or classrooms. Second, in VAM as in all nonexperimental causal modeling, one must consider the risk of omitted variables that might bias estimates of the effects in question. Our work shows that when VAM is applied to educational achievement, the risk of bias from omitted student characteristics depends on the characteristics of educational systems—specifically, the extent to which teachers or students with different characteristics are clustered in schools within and across years of testing. Third, VAM estimates are sensitive to the way achievement is measured, including the content of the tests and the methods used to put the results from successive grades onto a common scale.

Unfortunately, investigation and discussion of the issues raised by the use of VAM in education have been fragmented and incomplete. Although there have been reviews of one of the possible approaches (Bock, Wolfe, and Fisher, 1996), no reviews have carefully compared recent VAM efforts, and no papers have systematically discussed the wide variety of issues they raise. While numerous methodological concerns have been raised, much of the discussion remains unpublished, and the practical import of these concerns when VAM is applied to student achievement remains largely unclarified.

This document is one of the products of an effort by RAND Education researchers to begin a systematic review and evaluation of leading approaches to VAM. This work had several goals: to identify and explicate factors that could impact the validity of VAM references, to begin evaluating their practical impact, to spur additional work on these issues, and to help inform the debate among both researchers and policymakers about the potential of VAM. Other products from this project include a study of the variability in teacher rankings and the difficulties it creates for inferences about rankings (Lockwood, Louis, and McCaffrey, 2002). Another report presents a new model for VAM estimation and provides a detailed comparison of alternative statistical models used in VAM (McCaffrey et al., 2003).

In the following chapters, we clarify the primary questions raised by the use of VAM for measuring teacher effects, review the most important recent applications of VAM, and discuss a variety of the most important statistical and measurement issues that might impact the validity of VAM inferences. Although parts of this report are technical in nature, we have avoided lengthy discussion of technical issues. More-detailed discussion of technical issues is included as an appendix to this document (see the CD-ROM on the inside back cover) or can be found in the other products from the project.

We do not address the effects of VAM-based accountability systems on school and teacher performance in this document or in other publications resulting from this effort. We emphasize that this omission reflects only the limited scope of the present effort. Because VAM is being proposed as an approach for implementing accountability, it will be critically important to evaluate its actual effects on students, educators, and the quality of schooling. This evaluation should be central to ongoing research addressing the use of VAM.

CHAPTER TWO

What Are We Trying to Measure with VAM?

VAM purports to estimate the effect of educational inputs on student outcomes, in particular student achievement as measured by standardized tests. In this monograph, we focus on VAM applications to estimating teacher effects rather than schools because these applications have gathered the most recent attention. However, many of the issues we present pertain to any VAM application.

Measures of teacher effects are of interest as a means of answering at least two broad questions:

1. Do teachers have differential effects on student outcomes?
2. How effective is an individual teacher at producing growth in student achievement, and which teachers are most or least effective?

The first question requires estimates of the variability among teacher effects. If the data and statistical models can accurately describe the contributions of teachers to achievement, the models can provide estimates of the variability among teacher effects and determine the proportion of variability in achievement or growth that is attributable to teachers. The second question requires estimating individual teacher effects. As noted above, these estimates might be used to reward or sanction individual teachers on the basis of the teacher's performance relative to the distribution of teachers, possibly through ranking. The possible consequences tied to an estimated effect will determine the acceptable levels for the precision and accuracy of the estimate. Greater consequences require greater precision and accuracy.

Answers to these questions could have significant impact on both policy and practice in education. In this document, we present statistical and measurement issues that could affect the ability of VAM to answer one or both of these questions. We organize our discussion around the topics of general issues of statistical modeling, omitted variables, confounders and missing data, issues arising from the use of achievement tests as measures, and uncertainty about estimated effects.

Until recently, the effect of teachers on student performance has not been a primary focus of most attempts to improve education. Although studies showing significant variation among teacher effects date back to the mid 1970s (Hanushek, 1972; Murnane, 1975), for the most part these studies failed to influence policy debates or actions in a significant way. This lack of attention to teachers in policy discussions may be attributed in part to another body of literature that attempted to determine the effects of specific teacher background characteristics, including credentialing status (e.g., Miller, McKenna, and McKenna, 1998; Goldhaber and Brewer, 2000) and subject-matter coursework (e.g., Monk, 1994). These studies generally found that measured teacher characteristics were only weakly related to student learning, if at all.

In recent years, however, attention has increasingly focused on new research suggesting that teachers do in fact exert strong influence on student performance, and this research has already begun to shape debates about teacher training, professional development, and class assignments. In particular, several recent studies using VAM purport to demonstrate that teachers vary greatly in their effects on student learning. This evidence is consistent with the observations of most parents who have enrolled their children in school and who have encountered wide variation in the effectiveness of their children's teachers, and it has resulted in a growing consensus that teachers matter. These studies report that the effects of teachers may be even larger than those of socioeconomic status and other student background factors (Sanders and Rivers, 1996; Wright, Horn, and Sanders, 1997). At the same time, this research continues to fail to detect influence of specific teacher background characteristics on teacher effects (Rivkin, Hanushek, and Kain, 2000). Although the current research does not shed any light on the sources of variance among teachers, it does suggest—if the findings of large teacher effects prove accurate—that efforts to improve education for all students must address differences in effectiveness among teachers.

A few applications of VAM have measured individual teachers' effects and communicated these measures to the teacher and school administrators for the purpose of improving teacher performance. The most prominent, the Tennessee Value Added Assessment System, or TVAAS (Sanders and Horn, 1998) has produced effect estimates for teachers in grades 4–8 for the entire state of Tennessee since 1996. State law sanctioned this ambitious project and restricts the use of estimated effects in formal evaluations. The Dallas Independent School District also estimates teacher effects and uses these effects as a key component of teacher evaluations (Webster and Mendro, 1997).

The following sections provide a brief overview of some of the key issues in VAM. First we define the teacher effect and discuss some of the problems inherent in estimating it. Next, we discuss the importance of identifying the assumptions underlying any specific approach to VAM. Finally, we briefly discuss the kinds of student achievement measures that are necessary for appropriate application of VAM.

Teacher Effects

VAM teacher-effect estimates purport to measure a teacher's contribution to student achievement and learning. Teacher effects of this sort are what analysts refer to as *causal effects*. In lay terms, the teacher causes the effects. Conceptually, the teacher effect on a student is defined as the difference between the student's achievement after being in the teacher's class compared with his/her achievement in another plausible setting, such as with a teacher of average effectiveness.[1] Rubin (1974), Holland (1986), and West, Biesanz, and Pitts (2000) provide details on statistical models that formalize such causal modeling.

What Is a Teacher Effect?

Applications of VAM often model growth or gain scores as a means of measuring the effects of incremental inputs on incremental outcome—as the definition of value-added suggests (Hanushek, 1979).[2] Appropriate interpretation of VAM results requires that the causal effect be explicitly defined. Typically, there are multiple ways to define a causal effect, and some estimators can provide unbiased or consistent estimates of some causal effects but not of others. For example, Angrist, Imbens, and Rubin (1996) demonstrate that, under general assumptions, instrumental variable estimators provide estimates of the average causal effects of "treatment" on those who will take the treatment when it is offered. However, they do not necessarily estimate the causal effect of treatment on the entire population or on all people who were offered treatment. Alternative assumptions are required to make inferences about those causal effects.

When developing an explicit definition of a causal teacher effect, we must consider several particularly important issues. First, implicit in the notion of a *causal effect* is the comparison of a student's achievement with the current teacher with achievement under a plausible alternative. Unlike a new curriculum or program where there is often a well-defined single alternative such as the current curriculum, there is no single plausible alternative for a specific teacher's effect. We might consider other teachers as plausible alternatives. If so, which teachers: those in the same school, district, state? Or teachers who teach similar students regardless of location? And, if we choose

---

[1] Bryk and Weisberg (1976) use a similar notion for defining a value-added estimate of intervention effects in observational studies. They suggest comparing students to natural growth outside of the invention context, which is analogous to considering growth under an alternative teacher.

[2] Sometimes gains are implicit in the model, as is the case with TVAAS (Sanders, Saxton, and Horn, 1997; Ballou, Sanders and Wright, 2003; McCaffrey et al., 2003).

such teachers, do we then consider a particular alternative teacher or possibly an average of the alternatives? We might also consider no teacher as a plausible alternative. The appropriate alternative is likely to depend on the purpose for estimating teacher effects. In current applications, teacher effects are often estimated with respect to school district—so that the plausible alternative is implicitly the average teacher in the school district. Such a choice is appropriate for comparing teachers within a district but is inappropriate for ranking teachers in a state.

The definition of causal effect must also take into account which students are being considered. Teachers might not be equally effective with all students; some teachers may use methods that are most effective with high-achieving students, whereas others may be particularly skilled at improving the performance of struggling students. Similarly, some students might be more difficult to teach than others, which would affect VAM estimates to the extent that these students are distributed differentially across classrooms. For example, students reading well below grade level often have established habits and shortcuts that are barriers to learning to read and may require more work on the part of the teacher to achieve a certain amount of test-score gain. Thus, the effort expended by a teacher might not be proportional or linearly related to the resulting achievement gains, and this lack of a linear relationship could cause a teacher's effectiveness to vary with the student's level of achievement.

If teacher effects are not constant across students, then we need to be explicit about which effects we are considering. Again, an average effect might be appropriate. But which students should be averaged? All students in the population? Students likely to be taught by this teacher in the recent past and near future? Students in the teacher's class this year? The causal effect, as well as the validity of the estimate of the effect, will depend on this choice.

A teacher's effect might also depend on the context of the school or school district. For example, a teacher in a school with supportive colleagues or a cooperative principal might be more effective than in an alternative setting. Similarly, policies of a school district or school principal might influence a teacher's effect. For example, a school's choice of curriculum might change teacher effectiveness and improve student achievement and learning. In this case it is the action of the school combined with the teacher, rather than of the teacher alone, that has led to a change in the teacher's effectiveness. For some purposes, such as the evaluation of individual teachers, users of VAM results might want to make inferences about teachers that distinguish the teacher from her/his setting and school policies. For those applications, teacher effects that are partly a function of the school constitute a school effect. However, if users of VAM are interested in measuring the variability of teacher effects at a given time point and under the current context, the teacher effect of interest by definition includes, in part, the indirect effects of schools that affect students through teachers. Such indeterminacies led Meyer (1997) to conclude that estimating value-added teacher effects is impossible. Even if one does not agree with this pessimistic conclusion, these indeterminacies suggest that a precise definition should be explicit before any estimates are made.

A final issue in defining the teacher effect is the possibility that teacher effects vary over time. There is empirical evidence (Shkolnik et al., 2002; Rivkin, Hanushek, and Kain, 2000) that teacher effectiveness improves with experience during the early years of a teacher's career. Similarly, effectiveness may change as a result of modifications to class assignments or in response to factors outside of school. Kane and Staiger (2001) found considerable year-to-year variability in school test results. Again, if there is no single teacher effect, an explicit statement of the causal effect of interest is required. Choices might be the effect for the current year, the average effect during recent years, or the trend in the effect.

The appropriate definition of teacher effect depends on the question of interest, and no one definition will be appropriate for all purposes. For example, when considering the variability of teacher effectiveness in a given year, we might be interested in teachers' effects on the students they teach, and we may want to include indirect school effect as part of the teacher effect. But if teacher effects are to be used to sanction teachers, then we most likely would need effects that hold constant students and indirect effects from other sources such as the school or district.

Isolating the Teacher Effect

Even if the definition of the desired teacher effect is clear, it is important to recognize that VAM may not necessarily produce a pure measure of this effect. The current-year teacher is not the only source of variability in gain scores. Other educational factors, such as principal leadership, district-level policies, or prior teachers, might contribute to gains. Characteristics of the students, their environments, neighborhoods, families, and peers also contribute to gains, along with sources we might consider residual and measurement errors. Thus, although modeling gain scores avoids some problems associated with using single-year score averages to estimate teacher effects (see, e.g., Meyer, 1997) and might be preferable to modeling cohort-to-cohort test-score gains, models of gain scores do not necessarily measure the effects attributable to teachers. Growth might be the correct metric for measuring the importance of teacher effects, provided these effects are accurately and precisely estimated, but growth modeling is not sufficient to ensure that estimates are not confounded by other factors.

Some applications of VAM have used prior-year test scores as covariates in a regression model for current-year test scores rather than modeling gains. While covariate adjustments are often used to account for factors that might confound estimates of program effects in evaluations, simply controlling for prior-year scores and other available covariates does not guarantee that estimated teacher effects are causal effects.

In the evaluation literature, VAM and other studies that attempt to estimate causal effects in natural and uncontrolled settings are referred to as observational studies (West, Biesanz, and Pitts, 2000; Rosenbaum, 2002). Numerous methods exist for estimating causal effects from observational data. These include gain score and covariate adjustment methods (West, Biesanz, and Pitts, 2000), as well as other alternatives such as propensity score methods (Rosenbaum and Rubin, 1983) and selection models (Greene, 1997). However, all methods assume that models include or account for all variables that affect student achievement and differ across teachers. Any variables omitted from the model will continue to confound estimated teacher effects. Given the myriad of factors that are known or hypothesized to contribute to student achievement and learning and the fact that these factors often cluster by districts, schools, and classrooms, one of the greatest challenges for VAM is developing methods for separating the causal teacher effect from these other sources. As we discuss below, complex statistical models alone are not sufficient to guarantee that other factors do not confound estimated teacher effects, and sensitivity analysis and empirical investigations should accompany any estimated effects to demonstrate the robustness of estimates to other factors.

Comparing Teacher Effects to Alternative Notions of Teacher Effectiveness

We suggest defining a teacher's effect as *the average causal effect on student achievement across all students of interest.* This outcomes-based definition describes teachers only in terms of student achievement. It is not necessarily a meaningful characterization of other attributes of teacher effectiveness. As a somewhat extreme example but one that makes the point, suppose a teacher was very good at teaching test-taking skills to all students. This teacher would have a large positive effect because he was effective at teaching test-taking skills but he might not conform to other notions of effectiveness. If we are to make inferences about teachers, the outcomes-based definition of effects might be insufficient without additional investigations showing that positive effects correspond to other notions of effective teaching.

Along the same line of reasoning, the causal effect of a teacher alone does not give any indication of what makes a teacher effective. It provides no description of the practices, traits, or characteristics of teachers with large effects. Policies for improving teacher effectiveness require knowledge of the attributes that distinguish effective teachers from others. Knowledge that they can produce larger gains in student achievement than other teachers is not sufficient. Also, if empirical estimates of teacher effects do not correlate with other generally accepted traits of effective teachers, we might be concerned that our statistical estimation of teacher effects is too error-prone (due to sampling or systematic errors) to be useful.

Identifying Assumptions Required for Appropriate Application of VAM

Regardless of the definition of the causal teacher effect, most statistical models will produce unbiased or consistent estimates of a particular effect only when certain untestable assumptions hold. For example, the simple difference between the mean gain scores for a teacher's students and the mean for the entire school district provides an unbiased estimate of a teacher's effect—assuming that the teacher effect of interest is the average effect on all students, that students are essentially randomly assigned to the class, and that there are no school effects. Under other assumptions, this difference will estimate other causal effects or possibly provide a biased estimate that confounds true teacher effects with school effects or student characteristics. Unbiased estimation of the causal effect might require more-complex models than simple mean differences. Given a desired causal effect, the particular assumptions necessary for a statistical model for estimating that effect should be identified and evaluated for plausibility and formally tested, where possible. The impact of violations of assumptions will depend on the desired effect and the particular model. The sensitivity of estimates to assumptions is an area for extensive future empirical study.

Measures of Student Achievement

The causal effect of a teacher will depend on the measure of achievement. Effects on one measure of achievement will not necessarily equal effects on other measures. Users should choose a measure of achievement that suits the desired inferences. The most commonly used measures of student achievement are scale scores from standardized tests. However, these are not the only available measures. For example, criterion-referenced test scores that are not on a single developmental scale might also be used.

Summary

VAM refers to a class of models that are typically used to estimate the effects of teachers or schools on student achievement growth. The kinds of inferences that a particular application of VAM is intended to support must be taken into consideration when designing a modeling strategy. Although most discussions of VAM have focused on the magnitude of a "teacher effect," little attention has been paid to the various ways that such an effect may be defined. As we have discussed in this section, the definition of teacher effect involves the specification of a plausible alternative (e.g., the average teacher in the school, district, or state), as well as an indication of which students are being considered (e.g., all students in the population or students like those the teacher typically teaches) and what outcome is used to quantify achievement. The modeler must also determine whether the model is intended to distinguish school effects from teacher effects, and whether the current year or multiple years of teacher performance are of interest.

In addition to a definition of teacher effect, the use of VAM requires acknowledgment of the other factors influencing student achievement growth, including the characteristics of students, their environments, and their schools. Although VAM is intended to account for these factors, there is no guarantee that it does this adequately, and some models may address this more completely than others. Tests of sensitivity and robustness are important when interpreting the results of any VAM analysis.

CHAPTER THREE

Literature Review

The recent literature on VAM purports to show that teachers differentially affect student learning and growth in achievement. The reported effects are large, accounting for a significant portion of the variability in growth and persist for at least three to four years into the future. A relatively small number of papers—several not published in the peer-reviewed literature—are the source of these claims. In this chapter, we summarize and discuss the papers that make these claims. Our literature review is intended to be deep but not necessarily broad. Indeed, any education achievement model that uses gain scores or regresses current scores on prior scores could be considered a VAM, and we do not attempt to provide a comprehensive assessment of such research. Rather, we critically evaluate a modest number of research articles that were chosen because of their particular prominence and relevance to the scope of our project: VAM for estimating teacher effects. We organize our literature review by the primary findings of the studies: Teachers matter, teachers' effects are cumulative and enduring, and teacher effectiveness varies as a function of student achievement (see Table 3.1).[1]

---

[1] The methods used by the studies we reviewed correspond to different implied definitions of teacher effects as presented in Chapter Two. To ease presentation, we use the term *teacher effect* to refer to any variability in student scores that is attributable to teachers including indirect school effects, context effects, or variability of teacher effectiveness across students and time.

Table 3.1
Summary of Literature Reviewed

Teachers Matter	
Using diverse methods, these studies all purport to demonstrate the existence of teacher effects. The magnitude of effects and the relative importance of teachers compared with other factors influencing learning are difficult to assess, but our review suggests that these papers can be interpreted as demonstrating the existence of a teacher effect.	Papers reviewed: Wright, Horn, and Sanders (1997) Rowan, Correnti, and Miller (2002) Rivkin, Hanushek, and Kain (2000)

Teacher Effects Are Cumulative and Long-Lasting	
These studies purport to demonstrate the persistence of the effects of past teachers on future achievement. The consistency of the findings across studies, along with our analytical and simulation work, suggests that these papers can be interpreted as demonstrating the persistence of teacher effects. The magnitude of these effects, however, is possibly overstated.	Papers reviewed: Sanders and Rivers (1996) Rivers (1999) Mendro et al. (1998) Kain (1998)

Teacher Effects Differ by Level of Student Achievement	
This study purports to demonstrate that the lowest achieving students are the first to benefit from more-effective teachers. These findings are likely to result primarily from artifacts of the employed methods.	Paper reviewed: Sanders and Rivers (1996)

Within each of these three topics, we review the relevant papers separately. For each paper, we first provide a brief summary of the authors' conclusions and our critique of the paper. A detailed discussion of the study's research questions, methods, and results follows the summary. We then provide our critical evaluation of the methods and our assessment of the paper's results. At the end of each section, we summarize our conclusions for the topic addressed in that section. Although some of the reviews are lengthy—giving details on both the authors' methods and our critiques of those methods—the summary paragraphs will allow readers to follow the key points without reading the detailed discussion.

Teachers Matter

As we discussed previously, there is a long-standing debate over the effects of teachers on students, and VAM research has significantly shaped this debate in the past few years. Attention has recently been focused on a handful of studies that show residual variation at the classroom level and that interpret this variation as evidence of teacher effects. Three papers are particularly important in this area. First, Wright, Horn, and Sanders (WHS), in their 1997 paper "Teacher and Classroom Context Effects on Student Achievement: Implications for Teacher Evaluation," model student test score gains for two samples of schools from Tennessee. They consider multiple subjects and grades and measure the effects of teachers and a limited set of classroom contextual effects. They find that their teacher effect measure exceeds all other effect measures in 20 of 30 models they fit. Second, in "What Large-Scale Survey Research Tells Us About Teacher Effects on Student Achievement: Insights from the *Prospects* Study of Elementary Schools," Rowan, Correnti, and Miller (RCM, 2002) use the data from *Prospects*, a U.S. Department of Education–funded study of Title 1, to estimate teacher effects for three cohorts of students from a nationally representative sample of schools. They find moderate-to-large teacher effects depending on the model they fit. Finally, Rivkin, Hanushek, and Kain (RHK, 2000) use data from Texas schools to find a lower bound on teacher effects in their paper "Teachers, Schools, and Academic Achievement." They use a complex differences-of-differences approach as an attempt to estimate effects that do not confound student characteristics and teacher effects and find that teacher effects are nonzero.

One of the great challenges of estimating teacher effects is separating teacher effects from other sources of variability in student achievement, such as student background, peers, and neighborhoods, as well as school and school district or system inputs. The authors of these papers use a variety of models to attempt to uniquely identify the teacher effects.

Wright, Horn, and Sanders

Summary: WHS purport to show that teachers are the most important factor affecting student learning. In their replicated study design, they model gains in student test scores as a function of a small set of student covariates that include achievement and random teacher effects. They standardize the contributions of all variables in the models using what they call a "z-score." They informally meta-analyze the results of the 30 replicated models and find that the z-score for teacher effects exceeds the standardized contribution of every other variable in 26 of 30 models. Via a simulation study (see appendix for details) we find that standardized z-scores like those used by WHS do not necessarily preserve the ranking of variables based on their contribution to total variance in scores. In other words, while the WHS z-scores for teachers might dominate in 26 of 30 models, this does not imply that teacher effects explain more variance than all the other predictors. Furthermore, WHS provide no evidence that the estimated teacher effects and their corresponding variance components are unbiased by contributions of other inputs to education that are not accounted for in the model.

WHS replicate their analyses on data from two samples of Tennessee school systems. One sample contains schools from 30 school systems in East Tennessee and includes about 9,900 to 11,000 third graders, about 9,300 to 10,500 fourth graders, and about 6,500 to 8,900 fifth graders, depending on the outcomes. The other sample contains schools from 24 systems in Middle Tennessee and includes about 13,500 to 14,100, 12,300 to 13,500, and 8,600 to 10,100 third, fourth, and fifth graders, respectively, depending on the outcome.[2] For both samples, cohorts are identified by the students' grade in 1995—third, fourth, or fifth. For each sample, WHS model one-year gains in scale scores separately for each cohort (i.e., they model grade 3 less grade 2 scores, grade 4 less grade 3 scores, and grade 5 less grade 4 scores for each sample). They model the Tennessee Compre-

---

[2] WHS do not report on the number of schools, classes, or teachers included in the samples.

hensive Assessment Program (TCAP) math, reading, language, social studies, and science scores, fitting a total of 30 models: five subjects for each of three cohorts in each of two samples.

Although the authors led the development of the complex "layered model" used by TVAAS to simultaneously model test scores from multiple subjects and multiple years of testing on each student (Sanders, Saxton, and Horn, 1997), they do not use this model in the study at hand. Instead, they use a simpler and more traditional model of gains as a function of fixed effects for student and classroom characteristics and random effects for teachers. The model includes an overall effect for each teacher and additional terms to allow the teacher's effect to vary for students at different achievement levels (i.e., the model includes random teacher by student achievement-level interactions).[3] They include the following fixed-effect covariates: a student-level measure of average achievement equaling the average of the student's 1994 and 1995 scale scores (scores for second and third grade, third and fourth grade, or fourth and fifth grade, depending on the cohort) transformed into a four-level categorical variable with levels corresponding roughly to quartiles of the distribution of the continuous value; a classroom-level measure of heterogeneity equaling the standard deviation in achievement level (prior to categorization) grouped in the lowest quartile, the two middle quartiles, and the highest quartile and fit as a three-level categorical predictor; class size measured as either small (10 to 19 students) or large (20 to 32 students);[4] and indicators for school system.

The authors create a measure they call a "z-score" for each covariate in the model and teacher effects. In WHS (and our discussion of their paper), the term z-scores does not refer to common usages such as variables standardized to mean zero and variance one or test statistics. Rather, WHS use *z-score* to refer to a standardized regres-

---

[3] Teacher-by-achievement interactions are coded as deviations from the mean, so the teacher effect is the average teacher effect, and the individual interactions are teacher deviations from the average for each achievement group.

[4] Classes of less than 10 or more than 32 students were deleted from the study. See WHS for details.

sion parameter meant to measure the size of variable's effect on scores. For the random teacher effects and random teacher by achievement interactions, the z-score equals the estimated variance component for the effect divided by its estimated standard error. For the fixed-effects covariates, z-scores derive from a two-step calculation: First, p-values for the F statistics for testing the fixed effects are derived. Second, the z-score equals the quantile of a standard normal distribution corresponding to one less one half of the p-values (1– p-value/2). That is, the p-values from the F-test are treated as if they are p-values from a two-tailed test against the normal distribution. For example a p-value of 0.10 converts to 1.64 because $\Pr\{Z \leq 1.64\} = 0.05 = 1 - 0.10/2$.

The authors replicated their analysis 30 times and informally meta-analyzed the results by summarizing patterns in the results across models. The authors found that in their models for gains in achievement, the variance components for teacher effects were statistically significantly different from zero in all 30 models and students' average achievement was statistically significant in 26 of the 30 models (i.e., in 26 of 30 models they rejected the null hypothesis that expected gains scores were equal across the four achievement categories). Moreover, teacher effects had the largest z-score in 20 of the 30 models and achievement had the largest z-score in the remaining 10 models. The authors conclude that "the results of this study well document that the most important factor affecting student learning is the teacher" (WHS, p. 63).

While the authors clearly demonstrate that residual classroom variance is nonzero and by their metric has a large contribution relative to the other variables they consider, we believe that the conclusion that teachers are the most important factor should be made with caution. First, the authors provide no evidence that teacher effects and their associated variance measure the contributions of teachers and not other inputs to the education system. The authors include only a limited number of factors in the model and do not include factors such as school resources, the community, or student contextual effects. Some of the omitted factors might be significant and might contribute to the residual variance attributed to teachers. WHS give no details on the demographic distributions of students across schools and classrooms; as discussed in Chapter Four, the distributions of students determine the effect of omitted variables. Furthermore, because teachers are not randomly assigned to students, estimates may confound the teacher selection process with student effects. This could exaggerate empirical estimates of teacher effects. The authors do not measure contributions of schools or prior educational inputs. They also provide no information on the measurement properties of the TCAP and how the test corresponds to the curriculum of the various schools and school systems in the study. Nor do they discuss any variability in the importance of this test across teachers from different schools and school systems. As discussed in Chapter Four, all these factors might bias estimates of the variability among teacher effects. Without additional data, we cannot interpret residual classroom-level variance as a true measure of teacher effects.

Furthermore, as discussed in the appendix, unlike more-traditional measures of effect size, the authors' z-scores depend on the precision of estimates as well as true parameter values. Many factors can contribute to the precision of estimates and these can influence the z-scores. As a result, z-scores will not necessarily preserve the order in the relative magnitude of effects where effects are measured by a stable and interpretable alternative such as the share of the variance in gains scores explained by the factor. We used a simulation study to determine whether or not z-scores would tend to order variables according to the share of total variance they explain. We generated data using a model that included both teacher effects and covariates. In the model, the covariates and the teacher effects explained equal shares of the variance, so that across multiple models the z-scores for neither factor should dominate the other. The simulation study results found that under certain realistic settings, the z-scores for random teacher effects are likely to exceed the z-scores for fixed effects. Thus, the predominance of teacher z-scores does not guarantee the dominance of true teacher effects.

The conditions under which teacher-effect z-scores dominated other effects depended on the correlation between the variables and the true effect sizes. Greater correlation among variables results in a more likely dominance of teacher effects. WHS provide no discussion of the correlations among variables in the model. They also fail to provide the coefficients for the variables and the actual variability of the covariates among students. Therefore, we cannot compare the setting of the WHS study to the setting of the simulation study in which teacher z-scores artificially dominate the z-scores of other measure. We can only conclude that, without additional details, the dominance of z-scores provides no compelling evidence of the dominance of teacher effects. However, in our simulation studies, we found that z-scores for teacher effects of the magnitude reported in WHS are unlikely to result when residual classroom variance has no effect on scores. Thus, we believe that WHS provide evidence of residual classroom variance predicting gains, although we cannot evaluate the absolute or relative size of the effect given the information contained in the WHS paper.

Rowan, Correnti, and Miller

Summary: RCM find that residual classroom level variance accounts for a significant proportion of the variability in growth in student achievement scores. The results are robust across subject (reading or math), statistical model, and two cohorts of students from a nationwide sample of schools. Although all models result in classrooms accounting for meaningful portions of the variance, the magnitude varies. While the results are impressive, the authors do not provide details on missing data, the nature of the measure, and the distributions of student characteristics, so a full assessment of possible biases is impossible. Furthermore, we believe the authors' methods of calibrating the size of the effect of teachers might overstate teacher impact for one of their models.

RCM use data from two cohorts of students in the nationally representative sample of schools of the *Prospects* study. The students in the first cohort were tested twice in grade 1 and again in grades 2 and 3. Students in the second cohort were tested annually in grades 3, 4, 5, and 6. Analyses were conducted separately by cohort and in some cases by grade within cohort. The authors report that all analysis samples included at least 4,000 students from at least 300 classrooms, nested in more than 120 schools. The authors do not discuss the use of sampling or analysis weights or other methods used to account for the *Prospects* complex sample design.

For each subject, cohort, and grade, RCM fit four different models to the data to explore sources of variance in test scores. The first model is a three-level nested analysis of variance (ANOVA) with students within classes or teachers, classes within schools, and schools as the three sources of variance. The second model is a covariate adjustment model with a student's current year score equal to an additive linear function of prior-year score, teacher effect, school effect, student covariates, and residual error.

$$y_{ijt} = \alpha + \beta y_{ijt-1} + \gamma' x_{ijt} + \eta_{it} + \theta_{t(ij)} + e_{ijt} \tag{3.1}$$

where y_{ijt} is a math or reading score for the jth student in school i for test administration t; η_{it} is the school effect at this test administration; $\theta_{t(ij)}$ is the teacher effect for the student's teacher; x_{ijt} denotes a vector of student characteristics, some of which might vary over time; and e_{ijt} is residual error term. School and teacher effects are included as random effects.

The third model is a gain score model with a student's one-year gain in scores equal to a linear function of prior-year score, teacher effect, school effect, student covariates, and residual error. School and teacher effects are included as random effects. As noted in McCaffrey et al. (2003) and discussed in Chapter Four, because the gain-score model includes prior-year scores as an additive covariate in the model, this model is algebraically equivalent to RCM's second (covariate) model, and therefore we do not discuss this model in our review.

The final model fit by RCM is a cross-classified model (Raudenbush and Bryk, 2002). In this model, the score for the jth student in school i at time t, y_{ijt}, is given by

$$y_{ijt} = \alpha + \beta t + \delta t^2 + \alpha_i + \beta_i t + \alpha_{ij} + \beta_{ij} t + \\ \gamma' x_{ijt} + \theta_{1(ij)} + \ldots + \theta_{t(ij)} + e_{ijt} \tag{3.2}$$

where α_i and β_i are the random intercept and slope for the school; α_{ij} and β_{ij} are the random intercept and slope for the student; x_{ijt} denotes a vector of student characteristics, some of which might vary over time; $\theta_{1(ij)}$ to $\theta_{t(ij)}$ are the effects for the student's teachers at testing times 1 to t; and e_{ijt} is a residual error term. Thus, scores are models by a common quadratic function of time $(\alpha + \beta t + \delta t^2)$ plus school-specific and student-specific random linear time trends. The model assumes no variability in the nonlinear component of the model. Implicitly, any variation in δ is captured in the residual error term.

A teacher effect, $\theta_{t(ij)}$, is added for each year and these effects remain in the model undiminished at the future test administrations, which is why the model for the score at time t includes terms for all previous teachers. Although for convenience we refer to the term $\theta_{t(ij)}$ as teacher effects, RCM acknowledge that they are residual classroom effects. As shown in McCaffrey et al. (2003), the cross-classified model given above implies that

$$
\begin{aligned}
y_{ijt} - y_{ijt-1} = \beta - \delta + 2\delta t + \beta_i + \beta_{ij} + \\
\gamma'\,(x_{ijt} - x_{ijt-1}) + \theta_{t(ij)} + e_{ijt} - e_{ijt-1}
\end{aligned}
\tag{3.3}
$$

so the only teacher effect on gain scores is from the current teacher; other teachers do not contribute.

With the simple ANOVA model, RCM find that classrooms (including teachers) account for between 12 and 23 percent of the total variance in reading achievement and between 18 and 28 percent of the total variance in math achievement. In the covariate adjustment model, teachers (classes) account for 4 to 16 percent of adjusted variance in reading scores and 8 to 18 percent of adjusted variance in math scores, depending on cohort and grade. Adjusted variance is the residual variance after adjusting for student characteristics and prior scores.

For the cross-classified model, RCM find that variability in teacher effects accounts for 60 to 61 percent of "reliable variance" in growth in reading and 52 to 72 percent of the reliable variance in growth in math. RCM define *reliable variance* in growth as the variance of random school slopes, plus the variance in the random individual slopes, plus the variance in teacher effects. Variability in deviations around the linear trends is excluded from reliable variance.

RCM provide an important comparison of models using data from a national probability sample of schools. Replication of the analyses across cohorts and subjects (math and reading) consistently finds that teachers account for a nontrivial fraction of residual variance in all models for all cohorts and both subjects. However, we believe that the authors' use of reliable variance for defining the size of teacher effects from the cross-classified model might overstate the importance of teachers as a source of variability in gains in achievement. The analyses also have some limitations: *Prospects* data have a large proportion of incomplete student records, the inclusion of student characteristics and random school effects might bias the estimated effects toward zero, and measurement error is ignored in the covariate models. Also, because RCM is primarily a methodological paper that uses the *Prospects* study as a running example, the details they provide of their analyses are naturally limited and their interpretation of the results is constrained. For example, the authors provide no discussion on the measurement properties of the tests used in their study.

As noted above, RCM estimate the size of teacher effects from the cross-classified model as the ratio of the variance due to teachers to what they call the reliable variance. While we agree that calculation of size of the teacher effect should use reliable variance, we think alternative definitions of reliable variance might be preferable. Moreover, the authors' choice of measure of reliable variance provides the minimum value among alternatives. Thus, the authors' estimate of the size of the teacher effect is the largest it might be among alternative choices and might give an overly optimistic picture of teacher impact.[5]

---

[5]The issue in defining reliable variance is whether deviations around the linear trend constitute reliable variance or just idiosyncratic errors. RCM assume that all deviations from the linear trend are idiosyncratic errors that are not reliable measures of student growth. How-

The definition of reliable variance has a great impact on the size of the teacher effect. When all residual variance is included in the reliable variance, RCM find that teacher effects account for 13 to 14 percent of total adjusted variance in reading scores and 10 to 20 percent of total adjusted variance of math scores. These values are substantially less than the effect sizes they obtain based on their restrictive definition of reliable variance.

Including all the residual variance in the denominator is probably too extreme in that measurement error is included in the reliable variance, and it is not reliable by any standard. One alternative to the RCM definition is to reduce the residual variance in gains by a factor that accounts for measurement in the test and to add this adjusted residual variance term to RCM's reliable variance.[6] This alternative measure of reliable variance excludes variability resulting from the measurement process but includes the variability from all other nonlinearities. Ideally, we would go even further and fit random nonlinear growth curves that are smooth and then use the variability in these smooth curves for our measure of reliable variance. However, we cannot achieve this ideal with only a few data points per student. Thus, the best approach might be to estimate the RCM effect size based on both their measure of reliable variance (knowing it is an upper bound on the ideal) and our alternative (knowing it is a lower

---

ever, we believe that growth is naturally a nonlinear process, and—in accordance with other authors (Rogosa, Brandt, and Zimowski, 1982)—we view the linear growth model as an approximation to the true growth process. RCM appear to agree in that they include a quadratic term in their model (2.2). Just because terms are not linear does not mean they are not true features of student growth. Some portions of the deviations from linear growth are reliable in that they are not artifacts of the measurement process. If we tested students with two different test forms or near the same times, we would find that the deviations from linear trends that result from these alternative measures would be highly correlated. Also, just as linear growth is variable among students, the nonlinearities in growth are also likely to vary. Growth spurts will occur at different times and with different intensity for different students. We suspect that RCM exclude random quadratic terms from their model because they cannot be estimated reliably with data from just four test administrations—not because they believe there is no variability in the nonlinearities of growth. Thus, some of the variability in the residual terms is true variability in growth and should be included in the reliable variability of growth.

[6] The factor will depend on the standard error of measurement in tests, which must be obtained from external sources such as the test publisher.

bound on the ideal) and to present both. Without more information, we cannot determine a lower bound for the RCM estimates.

The *Prospects* data include many students with incomplete records of test scores (for some cohorts as many as 73 percent of records are incomplete—that is, 73 percent of students are missing a score for one or more tests) and RCM provide no details on how these records were used in the various analyses. We can assume that ANOVA and covariate models used only complete cases for each year because incomplete records cannot be used without imputation, and the authors did not mention imputation. Algorithms for estimating the parameters of the cross-classified model can use incomplete records without imputation; we assume that RCM used all available data when fitting these models. Modeling with incomplete records makes more-efficient use of the observed data and can provide unbiased estimates under weaker assumptions than can modeling with only complete cases (see the section "The Effects of Incomplete Records" in Chapter Four for details).[7] With the cross-classified model and for students who complete most of the tests, the model for the missing data probably deviates only minimally from the true distribution of the unobserved values. However, with such a large proportion of students missing scores and with students missing two or more tests, the effects of violation of the assumptions about missing data might be large. Without greater details about the distribution of students with missing data across classes and schools, we cannot speculate on the likely direction of that bias on estimates of the teacher variance component.

By including school effects and student covariates in their model, RCM might bias toward zero estimates of the teacher variance component. Random school effects should account for much of the school-level variance in scores, including any variance due to clustering of teacher effectiveness by school (see Chapter Four for additional discussion on this bias). Similarly, because the model includes fixed effects for student covariates but random effects for teachers, the

---

[7] The models treat the missing data as missing at random, MAR, rather than missing completely at random, MCAR, which is a more restrictive assumption (Little and Rubin, 2002).

model will overadjust for the student characteristics if true teacher effects are correlated with the average characteristics of their students. Assuming that teacher effects are positively correlated with the characteristics of their classes that are positively related to scores (i.e., more effective teachers teach the students who are likely to have larger growth in achievement), the overadjustment will result in biasing toward zero the teacher variance component.

On the other hand, the covariate adjustment model does not account for measurement error in prior-year scores, and the models almost certainly omit some variables that contribute to student scores. Both these limitations should tend to inflate the teacher variance component. But the models might mitigate such biases. The cross-classified model uses correlation among student scores to help offset the effects of omitted covariates (McCaffrey et al., 2003) and the inclusion of random school effects in the model should limit the confounding of teacher effects by school inputs and by the heterogeneity among the populations served by different schools.

On the whole, given the possible positive and negative bias in the estimates, we conclude that RCM provide convincing evidence of likely teacher effects, although the exact magnitude is less well established. Their results should be interpreted cautiously because effect sizes are relative to only part of the variability in scores (or growth) rather than to total variability.

Rivkin, Hanushek, and Kain

Summary: RHK take advantage of multiple cohorts of students, each with three years of test scores, to aggressively remove the effects of factors other than teachers that affect achievement. The authors find that teacher effects do exist and estimate that, as a lower bound, teachers account for about 3.2 percent of variance in achievement. In other words, a one-standard-deviation-unit increase in teacher effectiveness is associated with about a 0.18-standard-deviation-unit increase in scores. While the paper does remove many alternative factors, the estimates are based on differences of scores that are not on a single developmental scale. Therefore, changes in scores do not necessarily correspond to growth in achievement, which makes the interpretation of results difficult. Also, we conclude that the authors restricted their analyses to students who remain in the same school and complete testing for three consecutive years. Thus, the authors' finding suggests teachers can matter for some students in some metrics, but general interpretation of the results is impossible.

One of the primary limitations of WHS—and to a lesser extent RCM—is the possibility that residual effects of students or schools are not properly accounted for by the model covariates and therefore confound the estimates of teacher effects. RHK directly address this problem and attempt to estimate the true causal effect of teachers distinct from any other source of variability. RHK use data from over 500,000 Texas students from three consecutive cohorts attending 2,156 elementary schools. For each student they have linked math test scores for three years corresponding to grades 4, 5, and 6 for two cohorts and grades 3, 4, and 5 for the third. Students are linked to school by grade but not by classroom. The test scores are from the criterion-referenced Texas Assessment of Academic Skills (TAAS) test; therefore, across grades, scores are not measured on a single developmental scale. Rather, the authors standardize scores so that for each cohort at each grade, the average of the standardized scores equals zero and the standard deviation of the standardized scores equals one.

RHK use a complex method to separate teacher effects from other sources of variance in student scores. Consider a single school and let y_{ijg} denote the standardized grade g score for the jth student in cohort i. RHK first find gain scores

$$d_{ijg} = y_{ijg} - y_{ijg-1}$$

The authors note that by differencing scores, gains are uncorrelated with the effects of students, neighborhoods, peers, and schools on level of achievement. However, gains do not remove effects of these factors on growth. To remove the stable effect of these factors on growth, the authors difference gain scores from successive grades to obtain

$$a_{ij} = d_{ijg+1} - d_{ijg}$$

RHK then average the a_{ij} for the cohort to obtain A_i. The authors note that these averages depend on teacher effects for two grades:

$$A_i = T_{ig+1} - T_{ig} + residual$$

where T_{ig} is the average teacher effect for the teachers of the cohort at grade g and residual includes the effects of grades within school and terms unique to the student. An example of a grade-within-school effect is that the fourth grade curriculum might be better at promoting growth than the fifth grade curriculum, regardless of the teachers.

To remove these remaining confounding effects, the authors start by differencing A_i's from back-to-back cohorts and squaring this difference to obtain

$$D = (A_{i+1} - A_i)^2$$

Assuming that grade-within-school effects are constant across cohort, then D depends on $T^2 = \{(T_{i+1g+1} - T_{i+1g}) - (T_{ig+1} - T_{ig})\}^2$ and residual error terms. The authors note that if teacher effects exist, the square of this difference will tend to be small when teachers overlap between the cohorts and large when they do not. That is, across schools, T^2 and therefore D will vary with the teacher turnover rates for these cohorts.

To estimate the effects of teachers, the authors fit a linear regression model with D as the dependent variable and the turnover rate as an independent variable. They also include other school-level variables, such as change in district administration, and school fixed effects as the independent variables in some specifications of their regression model. The authors provide a mathematical derivation to recover the variance component for teacher effects from the coefficient for the turnover rate in this linear regression model.[8] The derivation assumes large samples of teachers per grade per school.

The authors find a statistically significant relationship between D and turnover rates in all of their models, regardless of additional covariates used to adjust for possible biases. Thus, the model indicates that cohort variability in differences of gains varies with teacher turnover. Under the assumptions of the authors' model, this implies that teachers affect gains in achievement as measured by standardized TAAS scores. The authors estimate that, as a lower bound, teachers account for about 3.2 percent of variance in achievement or that a one standard-deviation-unit increase in teacher effectiveness is associated with about a 0.18-standard-deviation-unit increase in scores.

This novel method cleverly uses the unique structure of multiple grades of scores for multiple cohorts to remove many sources of variability that might confound estimated effects. However, the method also has limitations. Most important, the estimate provides only a lower bound for the true variance component. In part, RHK provide a lower bound because the regression coefficient can be used to estimate the teacher variance component only up to a proportionality constant that is less than 1. However, the method also removes variance between schools and between school districts, which would serve to bias their estimates downward.

Another shortcoming of the method is that the relationship between D and the variance component of interest becomes exact only in the limit of large samples of teachers in each school. Most schools, however, have only a handful of teachers in any grade. With small samples, D will vary with teacher effects as well as with turnover rates. In particular, if average teacher effectiveness is related to turnover rates at schools, the estimate will be biased upward. Such a relation-

---

[8] The authors argue that the covariance between $(T_{i+1g+1} - T_{i+1g})$ and $(T_{ig+1} - T_{ig})$ is a function of the proportion, p, of teachers who teach both cohorts and the teacher effect variance component, τ^2. Under ideal settings that include large samples of teacher per grade per school, the D will grow linearly with p at a rate of $-4\tau^2$. Under less than ideal settings, the authors argue that D will grow linearly with p at a rate of $-4c\tau^2$ for an unknown proportionality constant, $c < 1$.

ship might occur if some schools can attract only the least-effective teachers and these teachers tend to quit after only a few years of teaching, while other schools are attractive to teachers and can hire and retain the most-effective teachers. School leadership, resources, and policies might contribute to such a scenario, and on its face the scenario is plausible. The authors add terms to their regression model to account for such bias but cannot guarantee it is removed.

The authors also assume that for any given grade, cohort-to-cohort variation in mean scores will not co-vary with omitted variables that might affect changes in both scores and turnover. For example, turmoil in schools or districts might lead to falling scores and high teacher turnover. Again, while the authors cannot test this assumption, the additional terms in their regression model including changes in principals and superintendents should offset some of the possible bias.

The authors do not discuss students with only partially complete test score data and scores from students who switch schools during the study. Given that the authors require three years of scores from a student to calculate a_{ij} and that their estimation procedure requires that a_{ij} not mix the effects of multiple schools, we suspect that the authors delete all student records with incomplete test score data and all records for students that change schools. Without details on missing data, we cannot assess the effect such a restriction might have on the estimated results. As discussed in Chapter Four, student mobility rates are high, so restricting the sample to complete records greatly limits the interpretability of the authors' findings.

The data used also limit RHK estimates. The lack of student-to-teacher links limits the utility of the data for directly estimating teacher effects, although the authors found a useful method to use the data to bound the teacher variance component. The lack of a developmental scale also makes interpretation more difficult. Gain scores are the key to the authors' analysis. However, the gains are not changes in achievement on a well-defined scale but rather changes in students' relative positions in the distribution of test scores. Given that the tests are not designed to measure a single scale, it is not clear that changes in the distribution reflect changes in achievement. Tests from different years might not measure the same skills, and changes in the relative position in the distribution might reflect differences in the skills measured by the tests rather than changes in achievement. Two students with equal gains on achievement might have different gains on the authors' measures. Of particular concern is the possibility that gains in achievement are correlated with levels of achievement during the first year of the study. If gains are positively correlated with initial levels of achievement, changes in relative position in the distribution could greatly overestimate gains for high- and low-achieving students. If gains and levels are negatively correlated the opposite might occur. This could distort variability among schools and bias the authors' results, but we cannot assess the possible magnitude or direction of such bias. Thus, we can conclude that the authors provide evidence of at least small teacher effects for gains measured by the standardized scores of students who remain in the same school for three consecutive grades, but we cannot assume these gains correspond to gains on a developmental scale.

Summary

Each of the studies reviewed in this section has limitations. WHS use a metric for comparing effects that is not guaranteed to preserve the ordering of effects and include only limited covariates in their models. RCM find generally consistent results across several models and cohorts in their study. However, most of their models include only a modest set of covariates, their data have large portions of incomplete records, and their procedure for standardizing effect sizes may overstate the importance of teacher effects in the cross-classified model. RHK difference standardized scores rather than scores from a developmental scale; their method relies on large sample results that do not directly apply to small samples of teachers in each school.

Despite these limitations, all three studies find that teacher effects matter. Our experience suggests that the limitations of the RCM study, in particular, should not result in sufficiently large bias to explain the observed teacher effects. The magnitude of effects and the relative importance of teachers compared with other factors influencing learning are difficult to assess, but our review suggests that these papers can be interpreted as demonstrating the existence of a teacher effect.

Teacher Effects Are Cumulative and Long Lasting

The studies discussed in the previous section sought to establish the importance of teachers to achievement of students in their classes. The papers discussed in this section attempt to establish the persistence of those teacher effects on students' future achievement. Sanders and Rivers (1996) use data from two school systems in Tennessee to study the cumulative effects of third, fourth, and fifth grade teachers on fifth grade math achievement. Rivers (1999) replicates this study using slightly different methods to measure the cumulative effects of fifth, sixth, seventh, and eighth grade teachers on ninth grade achievement. Mendro and colleagues (1998) replicate the Sanders and Rivers study using data from Dallas public schools, and Kain (1998) provides a separate independent reanalysis of the Dallas data.

Sanders and Rivers

Summary: In 1996, Sanders and Rivers released a technical report that purported to show that teacher effects accumulate over time. They report that for math tests, students taught by the least effective teachers for three consecutive years would score 52 to 54 percentile points below similar students taught by the most effective teachers for three consecutive years. This dramatic finding has garnered enormous attention from researchers, policymakers, and other interested parties. A web search found numerous references to this paper, and it has been cited several times in the peer-reviewed literature, though the paper itself has never been peer-reviewed. SR use ad hoc methods, which are difficult to assess and on their face appear likely to bias estimates of the persistent effects of teachers upward. We tested their method via an extensive simulation study and found that it is not guaranteed to result in positive bias in estimates of cumulative teacher (classroom) effects. Bias depends on many factors, including the true persistence of teacher (classroom) effects. Moreover, the method is unlikely to estimate persistent teacher effects when no teacher (classroom) effects exist. Simulations based on scenarios that best match numbers reported in SR and our experience with school data tend to show small positive bias in estimates of the size of the persistent effects of teachers (classrooms).

In the paper, Sanders and Rivers use a two-stage approach. First, they estimate teacher effectiveness using a form of the covariate adjustment model described in Chapter Four. The model assumes that current-year scores equal an additive linear function of prior-year score, the teacher effect, and residual error:

$$y_{it} = \alpha_t + \beta_t y_{it-1} + \theta_t(i) + e_{it} \tag{3.4}$$

where y_{it} is the ith student's math score at grade $t = 3$, 4, and 5, $\theta_t(i)$ is the teacher effect for the student's teacher at grade t, and e_{it} is residual error. Teacher effects are assumed to be random. Separate models are fit to math scores for third, fourth, and fifth grade students so that the coefficients of the model are allowed to change with grade. Also, any possible correlation among the residual errors from the same student is ignored. Teacher-effect estimates for each grade are grouped into quintiles to provide scoring of each teacher's effectiveness on a scale of one to five, with one assigned to teachers in the lowest quintile (least effective) and five assigned to teachers in the highest quintile (most effective). In the second stage, student scores from grade 5 are modeled as an additive linear function of teacher effectiveness (where the quintile assignments are treated as categorical variables) for grades 3 through 5, the second grade score, and residual error:

$$y_{i5} = \mu_5 + \beta_{5,2} y_{i2} + \sum_{g=3}^{5} \sum_{k=1}^{5} \gamma_{gk} T_{igk} + \varepsilon_{it}$$

where, for $k = 1$ to 5, T_{igk} equals one if student i's teacher in grade g has an effectiveness score of k and zero otherwise. The γ_{gk}'s denote the effects of teachers with a given effectiveness score. If some of the γ_{2k}'s and γ_{3k}'s are nonzero, then teacher effects persist in subsequent years testing. The same students are used in the first and second stages.

The authors' ad hoc method has been criticized for using the same students in both stages of the analysis (Kupermintz, 2002). On the face of it, the method appears to be circular—classes with low-scoring students are given low teacher-effectiveness scores and low teacher-effectiveness scores are found to be associated with low-scoring classes. However, the story is not so simple. Another way to view the two-step procedure is as a complicated way to estimate the size of a teacher effect; in that sense, the estimates are not reusing data but rather using the data to make the empirical estimate of interest.

We have shown through extensive analytic and simulation study that both perspectives have some merit. If the SR method is applied to just two years of data, then analytically we have shown that the estimates of differences between the students in the highest and lowest quintile are necessarily upwardly biased (see the appendix for details). However, when the method is applied to three or more years of data, the properties of the method cannot be assessed analytically. In these cases, we used a simulation study to determine the properties of the SR method for selected values of the parameters used to simulate student scores.

In the simulation study, we chose a model to simulate student scores and then applied the SR method to the simulated data. We compared the SR estimates of the effect of being assigned three of the most-effective teachers ($T_{g5} = 1$ for $g = 3$, 4, and 5) rather than three of the least-effective teachers ($T_{g1} = 1$ for $g = 3$, 4, and 5), to the true effect as determined by the data-generating model. The data-generating model had parameters for determining (a) the effects of teachers on students, (b) the persistence of teacher effects on future scores, and (c) the heterogeneity of classroom means of student effects and covariates, i.e., variables other than teacher effects that predicted scores. Thus, we had simulation scenarios in which, irrespective of teacher effect, classrooms would have different average scores or average gain scores. The study included cases with and without such heterogeneity in classroom means for student effects and covariates. Furthermore, some cases in the simulation allowed teacher effects to be correlated with student characteristics that differed across classes. The simulation also included cases in which student effects and covariates clustered by school but teacher effects were identically zero—i.e., there were no teacher effects. The details of the simulation study design are provided in the appendix.

The simulation study found no evidence that the SR method would necessarily be biased upward when more than two years of scores are modeled. With three or more years of data, bias depended very much on the true size of teacher effects and the persistence of those effects over time. If variance in teacher effects was extremely large relative to total variance (beyond what seems reasonable), bias in the method was always downward. That is, the method actually underestimated the deleterious effects of three ineffective teachers in consecutive years of school. When the variance of teacher effects was very small relative to total variance, the bias tended to be upward but often not large. When relative variance of teacher effects was moderate and in the range of estimates reported by SR and others, the bias tended to be small and slightly positive or negative depending on such issues as mixing of students among classes across grades and the true persistence of teacher effects. When teacher effects were at most weakly persistent into the future, the bias tended to be positive and inversely proportionate to the relative size of the variance of the teacher effects—the smaller the relative variance of teacher effect, the larger the positive bias.

Generally, the results of the simulation were similar for cases with and without heterogeneous classroom means for student effects and covariates—the method was not necessarily biased in either direction when multiple years of data were used. However, correlation between teacher effects and student covariates resulted in greater and more-consistent positive bias. In particular, when the variance in teacher effects was small relative to total variance, the SR method always produced positive bias.

For many plausible settings of the simulation parameters, the simulation study found positive bias for the SR method. In cases that our experience suggest are most plausible (in part because they provide estimates that are similar in magnitude to those reported in SR), the bias in the SR method appears to be about 20 percent when comparing student outcomes after three years with the most-effective teachers to outcomes after three years with the least-effective teachers. In these cases, the teacher effects are small to moderate (0.033 to 0.13), weakly persistent, and correlated with student characteristics that affect achievement and cluster within schools. The bias is highly sensitive to the persistence of such effects. If the teacher effects do not persist, the bias could be considerably larger. On the other hand, if the teacher effects are strongly persistent, the bias is likely to be about zero.

Our simulation results indicate that the SR results are unlikely to occur if teacher effects are truly zero. Only under seemingly implausible values of design parameters could we produce results as large as those reported by SR when teacher effects were truly zero. When classroom means of covariates or student effects were heterogeneous, the SR method consistently estimated positive cumulative effects of teachers even though teacher effects were identically zero by design. However, the estimated effects were smaller than the effects reported in SR except when student covariates had exceptionally large effects on scores or gains—effects that were inconsistent with values reported in empirical studies of the effects of student characteristics on test scores.

The teacher effects in our simulation could represent in real data either true teacher effects or classroom effects resulting from factors other than individual student effects or characteristics. Such classroom effects might arise, for example, from interactions among students. Thus, our simulation study investigates possible bias in the SR method in estimating the persistence of teacher and classroom effects. Our simulation cannot address the SR method's ability to distinguish teacher effects from classroom effects. Because SR provides no discussion on distinguishing teacher effects from classroom effects, we can conclude only that the method is likely to result in small bias in estimates of the cumulative effects of teacher *or* classrooms.

SR provide no discussion of the measurement properties of tests used in their study, nor do they provide any discussion of missing data. The test score data are from the TVAAS database and are therefore scaled scores. However, only students who complete all four grades of testing can have the complete data required to fit the model. Bias from excluding incomplete records is difficult to assess without any data on the number and distribution of students with missing scores across schools and teachers. Thus, given our simulation and analytic results and the lack of information on missing data, we cautiously conclude that for students who are likely to complete testing, SR provide evidence of the existence and persistence of teacher or classroom effects, but the size of the effects is likely to be somewhat overstated.

Rivers

Summary: Given the magnitude of SR's effects, the implications of this finding, and the controversy with the methodology, other authors have attempted to replicate the result with slight modification. Rivers (1999) replicates the design with several important changes to address some of the criticisms of SR and still found persistent teacher effects. Because of possible spurious correlation between classrooms and student outcomes and because of measurement error in the covariate grade four test scores used as a covariate adjustment, Rivers' results might have positive bias that we suspect would be small to at most moderate.

Rather than use SR's simple covariate adjustment model (Eq. 3.4) to estimate teacher effectiveness, Rivers uses the teacher-effect estimates from the TVAAS model. As discussed in Chapter Four, the TVAAS is a complex model of the joint distribution of longitudinal student test score data. It simultaneously models scores for up to five subjects (math, reading, language, science, and social studies) for up to six years of testing. The model implicitly uses gain scores for estimating teacher effects. Although it includes no student, classroom, or school-level characteristics, the model allows for correlation among scores from the same student, and this at least partially adjusts for the omitted student characteristics. The TVAAS model includes a separate parameter for the mean of every school system or district; so estimated teacher effects are relative to the other teachers in the district. (See Chapter Four and McCaffrey et al. (2003) for details on the TVAAS model and in particular the effects of omitting covariates from such models.)

The second difference between Rivers and SR is that Rivers used two cohorts of students rather than one to estimate the persistence of teacher effects. The first cohort provided estimates of teacher effectiveness from the TVAAS model. The second distinct cohort of students provided estimates of the impact of teacher effectiveness. Rivers conducted the stage 2 analysis of SR on the second cohort. She models ninth grade test scores as a function of fourth grade test scores and the students' fourth to eighth grade teachers' stage 1 effectiveness ratings based on the prior cohort. Thus, estimates of teacher effectiveness and the impact of varying effectiveness were estimated from two distinct cohorts of students.

The final major difference between Rivers and SR is that Rivers models outcomes on a different test than the test used for estimating effectiveness, and the outcome is measured at the end of ninth grade while teacher effects are measured for sixth, seventh, and eighth grades.

Rivers models scores on the TCAP math competency test administered in the fall of ninth grade for all 2,612 students in two Tennessee school districts who completed both the ninth grade TCAP math competency test and the fourth grade TCAP math achievement test. The model assumes that ninth grade scores are a linear function of (a) district means, (b) fourth grade math scale score, (c) within-district quartile of the fourth grade scale score coded as three indicator variables, (d) an interaction between fourth grade scale score and district, (e) TVAAS estimated effects for the students' fifth, sixth, seventh, and eighth grade teachers, and (f) interactions between the students' fourth grade math scale score and their fifth and sixth grade teachers' effects, and residual error.

Rivers finds that teacher effects from all four grades are statistically significantly related to scores in the fall of ninth grade. The effect of fifth and sixth grade teachers decreases with the students' fourth grade scores. That is, fifth and sixth grade teachers were estimated to matter more for students with lower baseline scores. The impact of fifth grade teachers on ninth grade tests is about two times greater for students at the mean of the lowest quartile of fourth grade scores than the impact for students at the mean of the highest quartile. The impact of sixth grade teachers is about 2.5 times greater for students in the lowest quartile compared with the highest quartile on the fourth grade test.

Rivers found that for students scoring low at fourth grade, fifth and sixth grade teachers had the strongest relationship with ninth grade scores, while for other students, eighth grade teacher effects had the strongest relationship with ninth grade scores. Rivers gives values for the effect sizes of ineffective and highly effective teachers in each grade. The difference between the expected grade 9 scores for students taught by a highly effective teacher compared with those taught by an ineffective teacher in a particular grade ranged from about 15 percent of a standard deviation unit to about 43 percent of a standard deviation unit depending on the grade and the students' fourth grade scores. The difference for eighth grade teachers was 24 percent of a standard deviation unit.

As discussed in Chapter Four, measurement error in the fourth grade scores can bias estimates of all the coefficients in the model. Without additional details, we cannot hypothesize on the likely direction of that bias. However, given that the fourth grade test is a form of the Comprehensive Test of Basic Skills (CTBS) standardized test, the reliability is likely to be high and the bias unlikely to be large enough to completely explain the observed coefficients for teacher effects.

As discussed in McCaffrey et al. (2003), teacher-effect estimates can be confounded by student characteristics that vary across schools when few students transfer across schools. These confounding effects are likely to remain constant across time, creating a possible spurious correlation between teacher effects estimated with a previous cohort and scores with the current cohort. The inclusion of fourth grade scores as covariates in Rivers' model should mitigate, but not necessarily remove, such spurious correlation between measures of teacher effectiveness and student scores. Without greater details on the distribution of student characteristics across schools, we cannot assess the likelihood of such possible spurious correlation. Although we did not conduct a simulation study of Rivers' methods, our simulation study of the SR method (described in the subsection above on Sanders and Rivers and in the appendix) describes the effects of spurious correlation on estimates on the effect and persistence of effective teachers. The results of that simulation study suggest that the spurious correlation between effectiveness measures and student outcome is likely to lead to the positive bias in Rivers' estimates when teacher effects are small to moderate, persist weakly over time, and correlate with student characteristics. Note, however, that because only the teacher and not the classroom remains constant across cohorts, unlike SR, Rivers' estimated teacher effects should be distinct from classroom effects.

Rivers' results apply only to students who remained in the school district for over five years and who completed testing at grades 4 and 9. The study excludes transfers and students retained in grade. How results for these students might differ compared with results for all students is unknown. In addition, TVAAS teacher effects and Rivers' models are relative to the district mean. If teacher effectiveness differs across districts, Rivers' results could underestimate the impact of teachers on later grades.

Thus, on balance, Rivers' study provides evidence that, for students who remain in the same school systems for six years, teachers affect achievement on standardized tests taken several years in the future. Because of possible spurious correlation and measurement error in the baseline score, Rivers' results might have positive bias that we suspect would be small to at most moderate. Also, because teacher effectiveness might tend to cluster by district, Rivers' results might also be biased toward zero for inferring the effects of teachers across large units of aggregation. such as counties, metro areas, or states.

Mendro, Jordan, Gomez, Anderson, and Bembry

Summary: Mendro, Jordan, Gomez, Anderson, and Bembry, (MJGAB, 1998) use data from students in the Dallas Independent School District to replicate the SR study. Although the Dallas model for estimating teacher effects controls for many covariates, MJGAB—unlike the models of SR and Rivers—consistently find large persistent teacher effects across multiple cohorts and on both reading and math scores. The authors provide insufficient details on their model results, the extent of incomplete student records, and the psychometric properties of their test for us to completely evaluate the accuracy of their estimated values, but their study is valuable because they corroborate the results of SR and Rivers, even with a very different approach.

MJGAB analyze data from five cohorts defined by grade in 1997: fourth graders (with data from grades 1–4); fifth graders (with data from grades 1–5); sixth graders (with data from grades 2–6); seventh graders (with data from grades 3–7); and eighth graders (with data from grades 4–8). They conduct four separate analyses on these cohorts. The first analyzes math scores from all students with four complete years of math scores. The second analyzes reading scores from all students with four complete years of reading scores. The third and fourth analyses replicate these analyses, restricting the sample to all students with five complete years of test scores in reading or math. Fourth graders are excluded from the last two analyses. All analyses use the Iowa Test of Basic Skills (ITBS) survey form as the measure of achievement.

The authors use teacher-effect estimates from the Dallas Value Added Accountability System (DVAAS). DVAAS uses a three-stage approach to estimating teacher effects. In stage 1, it removes the effects of so called "fairness variables" from current-year and past-year scores and attendance rates. The fairness variables are ethnicity-language proficiency (limited-English proficient—LEP, black [not LEP], Hispanic [not LEP], and other), gender, free-lunch status (two levels), and first- and second-order interactions of these three variables. The fairness variables also include census-block level measures of income, poverty, and college attendance (defined at census-block level for the student). For current-year and prior-year reading and math scores, DVAAS fits linear models to predict the scores from the fairness variables. It retains residuals from these models for the next stage of estimation. The residuals are standardized within strata defined by the regression model's predicted values for the outcome. Webster and Mendro (1997) provide details of the standardization.

Stage 2 of the DVAAS estimation procedure models the first-stage residual for the current-year score as a function of first-stage residuals for prior-year scores, prior-year attendance, and school-level variables. The model also includes interactions between the school-level variables and the residuals for the prior-year outcomes. School-level variables included in the model are school-level mobility, crowdedness, percentage minority, percentage black, percentage Hispanic, percentage free lunch program, and the averages of the census-block level fairness variables. The model also includes random school effects and random slopes on predictor that vary by school (stage 1 residuals for prior-year outcomes and attendance). The residuals for individual student scores from the stage 2 models are called stage 2 residuals and are saved for the final stage of estimation.

Stage 3 estimates teacher effects as the classroom averages of the stage 2 residuals. The procedure produces separate estimates for teacher effects on the ITBS math and reading scores. Details on the Dallas teacher effects are presented in Webster and Mendro (1997).

MJGAB use the final stage 3 estimates as their measures of teacher effectiveness. For the analyses with four years of data, teachers are given ratings of one to five corresponding to the quintile of their stage 3 estimated effect, with one denoting the smallest effects and five denoting the largest. For the analysis with five years of data, teachers were sorted by the size of their estimated effects and grouped into three roughly equal size groups numbered one, two, and three from smallest to largest effects. A teacher's rating equaled the group number.

MJGAB begin by fitting models analogous to those of SR. The models include pretest scores as a covariate, and they include teacher ratings for each of three or four years depending on the analysis. Teacher ratings are included in the model as a series of four or two indicator variables depending on whether there are five or three rating values. MJGAB do not report the models but state that teacher effects were highly significant.

The authors also note that students taught by an ineffective teacher in one year do not make up for this loss even after additional years of schooling. They demonstrate this effect by showing outcomes (means for normal curve equivalents or percentile) for pairs of groups of students. The pairs have similar average percentiles on the pretest, but one group in each pair had ineffective teachers in the first year (after the baseline), while the other group had effective teachers. The authors present 18 such pairs; regardless of the effectiveness of the teachers in the ensuing years, the group with an ineffective teacher in the first year always scored lower on the final test. The authors present results for both reading and math and for students with both four and five years of data. The consistency of these results is impressive, but the authors do not present sample sizes and they had many groups from which to choose. They do not discuss how many comparisons, if any, contradicted these findings.

Kain (1998) reanalyzed a subsample of the data used by MJGAB. He used data through 1996 for students with four complete years of data to that point. He fit linear models using 1993 scores and the teacher-effect ratings for 1994, 1995, and 1996 as covariates in his models. His models were linear in the teacher ratings. He repeated the analysis using scale scores and the natural log of the scale scores. He found that teacher effects for every year were statistically significant predictors of final-year scores. The results were similar across grades and subjects and were not sensitive to transformations of the outcome.

Neither Kain (1998) nor MJGAB made any corrections for measurement error in the pretest scores and this could result in bias in the estimates for the other coefficients. Also, the results do not apply to students who transfer or miss testing for other reasons. Furthermore, they do not provide sufficient details on their results for a careful evaluation of the estimated effects. The value of these papers is in corroborating of the results of SR and Rivers. Kain and MJGAB use a very different stage 1 approach than SR and Rivers do. Their stage 1 model aggressively removes covariates—possibly overcorrecting estimated teacher effects if true teacher effectiveness is correlated with the characteristics of the students they teach. However, the authors find that teacher effects persist. This result was determined independently by Kain and MJGAB and was robust to nonlinear transformations of the outcome measure. Moreover, because the MJGAB and Kain analyses control for many student characteristics, including neighborhood effects, the estimated teacher effect should be relatively unconfounded by other classroom effects.

Summary

Overall, the consistency of results across SR, Rivers, MJGAB, and Kain, combined with our simulation study of the SR methodology, suggest that teacher effects from prior years are correlated with future test scores—even several years later. The size of the effects is possibly overstated in SR, but our simulation study suggests that SR's results are unlikely when true effects are zero. Rivers removes the confounding of teacher and classroom effects and also finds persistent effects. The findings of MJGAB and Kain, which control for many student variables, further support interpreting these results as due, at least in part, to teachers.

Teacher Effects Differ by Level of Student Achievement

Summary: SR explore not only the cumulative effects of teachers but also how teacher effectiveness varies with the level of student achievement. They purport to show that students from the lowest level of achievement are the first to benefit from more-effective teachers. However, we determined that the authors' findings are artifacts of the analysis and cannot be interpreted as measuring interactions between teacher effectiveness and student achievement.

To study the issue of the differences among students in the impact of teacher effectiveness, the authors classify grade 5 students by grade 5 teacher quintiles (as defined above) crossed with the student's level of achievement. Level of achievement equals the average of the fourth and fifth grade scale scores grouped into four categories defined by 50-point intervals from 650 to 849. Within each cell of the cross-classified table, SR report the mean gain score. They repeat the table for each of the two districts used in their study.

The authors find that within each level of student achievement, average student gains increase with teacher effectiveness. The table also shows that within each quintile of teacher effectiveness, gains are negatively related to achievement—students with the lowest level of achievement make the greatest gains. The authors interpret this finding as indicating that students with the lowest levels of achievement are the first to benefit from more-effective teachers.

The table cells and cell means depend on three variables for each student: $r = y_5 - by_4$, $d = y_5 - y_4$, and $m = (y_4 + y_5)/2$, where y_4 and y_5 denote the fourth and fifth grade scale score respectively and b equals the estimated regression coefficient from the model predicting fifth grade scores from fourth grade scores. Teacher effects depend on the class mean of r.[9] Achievement is defined by m and cell means equal the mean of d.

The three variables r, d, and m are linear combinations of just two scores, y_4 and y_5. Therefore, ignoring the sampling error in b, conditional on any one variable the other two variables have correlation 1 or −1. It is straightforward to show that, conditional on m, the correlation between r and d is positive when $b > 0$—that is, when fourth and fifth grade scores are positively correlated, which almost surely holds for the SR study. Conditional on r, d and m are negatively correlated when b is less than 1. The coefficient b is less than 1 when scores "regress toward the mean," so that students who score at the extremes in fourth grade tend to be less extreme in fifth grade. Regression to the mean is nearly universal in test scores, so we feel confident that b is less than 1 in the SR data for both districts.

---

[9]Because SR use the best linear unbiased predictors (BLUPs) to estimate teacher effects, the teacher effect equals the classroom mean pulled back or shrunken toward zero to reduce variance in the estimated effect. The amount of shrinkage toward zero depends on the number of students in the class. The fewer the number of students, the greater the shrinkage (Searle, Casella, and McCulloch, 1992).

Thus, the positive correlation between quintile and gains conditional on achievement is likely an artifact of the perfect positive correlation between r and d conditional on m. Likewise, the negative correlation between gains and achievement level conditional on teacher quintile is likely to be an artifact of the perfect negative correlation between d and m conditional on r. The findings are difficult to interpret because of structural relationships between these variables. Alternative analysis strategies are necessary if one wishes to explore the important questions about how teacher effects vary with student achievement.

CHAPTER FOUR

Modeling Longitudinal Data to Estimate Teacher Effects

Estimating the effects of teachers by modeling longitudinal data on student achievement raises a number of important statistical and psychometric issues, some of which require analyst decisions. These are partially overlapping, but for clarity, we break them into four groups: basic issues of statistical modeling; issues involving confounders, omitted variables, and missing data; issues arising from the use of achievement test scores as dependent measures; and uncertainty about estimated effects.

Our considerations of these issues are made with respect to criteria about how useful estimates of teacher effects should behave. As discussed in Chapter Two, we assume that analysts have defined true teacher effects in a way that is reasonable for their intended uses. Questions about estimator performance then center around a few key principles. First, statistical estimates of teacher effects should be close to the true effects, however they are conceived. Second, estimates should be relatively invariant to different plausible estimation procedures or modeling choices; if estimates vary appreciably across models, the resulting uncertainty of findings should be considered (Lindley, 2000). Finally, to the extent that estimated effects deviate from true effects, these estimation errors should not be related to characteristics of students or teachers or other identifiable factors. Correlation between estimation errors and student characteristics, for example, would undermine the motivating purpose of VAM, which is to isolate teacher effects from other factors affecting student achievement.

In the following sections, we discuss in detail a number of circumstances and analyst decisions that may affect the ability of statistical estimates of teacher effects to achieve these ideals. Some of the issues require somewhat esoteric discussions of technical details. Table 4.1 organizes the issues presented in this chapter. In addition, we summarize the key points in a paragraph at the beginning of each section to allow readers to ascertain the key points without reading all the technical discussion.

General Issues of Statistical Modeling

In this section, we discuss the choice of a basic model for analyzing scores and the specification of teacher effects as either fixed or random. The following sections describe some models commonly used in VAM to estimate teacher effects and variance components. This discussion is predicated on the assumption that the analyst has data to support VAM and models must be sensitive to the available data. The unique feature of VAM is the use of longitudinal data on students to estimate teacher effects. Thus, the data system must include test scores from multiple grades for individual students. The test should have well-established psychometric properties and measure the attributes of interest. For example, a test of basic skills might be inappropriate if the analyst is interested in estimating a teacher's effectiveness at teaching advanced skills. The database must also contain links between students and their teachers, schools, and school districts including data on team teaching. Inclusive data tracking systems that follow students across schools and districts will limit the number of students who are missing some test scores. In addition to scores and linking information, the ideal data would include a large number of variables describing student background demographic, socioeconomic, family, and neighborhood characteristics. In reality, these data often are limited to a small number of variables such as race-

Table 4.1
Factors That Can Influence VAM Estimates

General Issues of Statistical Modeling

Analysts must choose among the alternative modeling approaches that are available for VAM estimation. We discuss the alternatives and present relative strengths and weaknesses.	Specific topics covered: Basic models for analyzing achievement gains Specification of teacher effects as fixed or random

Omitted Variables, Confounders, and Missing Data

Many factors other than the current year teacher influence student achievement. Also, longitudinal data often are incomplete. We discuss the implications of omitting or incorrectly specifying factors in models for teacher effects and the impact of missing data.	Specific topics covered: Importance of the inclusion of student background variables as covariates Disentangling school and district effects from teacher effects Disentangling the effects of earlier teachers and schools from estimated teacher effects The effects of incomplete records Linking students to teachers

Issues Arising from the Use of Achievement Tests as an Outcome

Student achievement is measured imperfectly by tests, and alternative test constructions can change inferences about achievement. We discuss choices in timing of measurement and test construction that might influence inferences about teachers.	Specific topics covered: The effects of timing of tests Issues posed by the construction and scaling of tests Inflation of test scores Using achievement measures as a proxy for measures of teacher effectiveness Modeling in the presence of measurement error

Uncertainty in Estimated Effects

Errors in estimated effect arise from variability in the students' score as well as uncertainty about the appropriate statistical model. We discuss the implication of both sources of errors.	Specific topics covered: Sampling error Other sources of uncertainty

ethnicity, native language, and participation or eligibility for free or reduced price lunches. Finally, additional information about teachers and schools, such as professional preparation and educational resources, could also be beneficial.

Basic Models for Analyzing Achievement Gains

Summary: Analysts generally have used one of three approaches to analyzing longitudinal data to estimate teacher effects: "covariate adjustment models" that regress current scores on prior scores; "gain scores models" that treat successive-year gains as outcomes; and "multivariate models" that directly model the full joint distribution of all student outcomes. Because of differing assumptions, the three approaches have different strengths and weaknesses, and none is superior under all circumstances. In general, however, as a statistical model for estimating teacher effects, the multivariate model will often be preferable because of its flexibility and efficient use of the available data.

VAM seeks to determine the effects of incremental inputs—in the case we consider, the incremental effects of teachers—on educational achievement, accounting for prior achievement. This endeavor is challenging because students exhibit growing achievement during exposure to changing environments (e.g., different teachers' classrooms.) Analysts have generally used one of two broad approaches for analyzing longitudinal data from students to estimate teacher effects. The first approach, which itself subsumes two distinct classes of models, separates the analysis of the longitudinal data into a sequence of univariate problems where the outcome measures and students are nested within classes each year. The other approach is to model simultaneously the joint distribution of all measurements, as well as the changing environments in which those measurements are made. Although all these modeling approaches are in some sense multivariate, when discussing the approaches below, we use the term "univariate" for the former approach (sequentially modeling single outcomes) because the outcome is univariate, and we use the term "multivariate"

for the latter approach (jointly modeling multiple years of scores) because the outcome is multivariate.

The two classes of models comprising the univariate approach
are what we term "covariate adjustment models" and "gain score
models." Covariate adjustment models specify the current score as a
function of the prior score and possibly other covariates, using separate models for each year and explicitly linking students' scores to the
effects of their current teachers only. These models could take any
number of forms, but the common ones specify current scores as linear functions of the covariates. We use the term to refer only to models that assume linearity, except where specifically noted otherwise.
Rowan, Correnti, and Miller (2002), Sanders and Rivers (1996), and
DVAAS (Webster and Mendro, 1997) are recent examples of the covariate adjustment approach. This approach has a long history for
modeling education production functions, including estimating
teacher effects (see Hanushek, 1972; Murnane, 1975).

The covariate adjustment model assumes that

$$y_t = m_t + b y_{t-1} + T_t + e_t \qquad (4.1)$$

where y_t denotes the student's score at time $t = 1, 2, \ldots, p$, m_t is a
student-specific mean that might depend on student characteristics
and other variables, T_t are teacher effects, and e_t are residual errors
that are assumed to be Gaussian (normally) distributed and independent of y_{t-1} and the teacher effects. The models are fit separately
for each year of data so that the only use of information from multiple years is through the prior-year covariate.

Alternatively, gain score models specify a one-year gain score
(current score less prior score) separately for each year and link student gains to their current-year teacher's effects. In recent VAM
models (e.g., RCM), these gains have been measured from spring of
one grade to spring of the next, although one might also measure
gains from the start of a grade until its end. Specifically the gain score
model assumes:

$$y_t - y_{t-1} = m_t + T_t + e_t \qquad (4.2)$$

where the terms are analogous to those for the covariate model. Again, the residual errors are assumed independent of the teacher effects and Gaussian (normally distributed). Because each year is modeled separately, estimated effects cannot use information from multiple years.

Both the covariate adjustment and gain scores models might treat the teacher effects as fixed or random (see next section) and may include covariates as part of the specification of m_t. To keep the notation simple, we often use the same notation for analogous terms (e.g., the mean or the teacher effect) from the various models presented in this section. This reuse does not imply that the terms are equal across models.

There has been a substantial and long-standing debate over the use of gain scores or covariate adjustment models (see for example, Thum, 2003; Rowan, Correnti, and Miller, 2002; Rogosa, 1995; Allison, 1990; Bryk and Weisberg, 1977). Lord (1969) showed that even in simple situations, the two methods may give different results. The two approaches describe the dynamic system of student learning differently, and thus neither is necessarily correct for any application or consistently "better" than the other. As noted by Bryk and Weisberg (1977), ". . . the choice of an appropriate analysis method is highly sensitive to assumptions about the nature of individual growth." Because both approaches can perform poorly for some models of growth, Bryk and Weisberg (1976 and 1977) and others (see Rogosa and Willett, 1982) suggest modeling growth rather than using these two more common approaches. We do not advocate one method over the other as a means of estimating teacher effects, but rather list the relative advantages and disadvantages of each method later in this section.

The second major analytical approach for estimating teacher effects, which we term "multivariate modeling," is distinctly different from either of the univariate approaches. Multivariate models directly specify a joint distribution for the entire multivariate vector of scores for the student. The models express the score means as a function of time, specify the variances and correlations between pairs of scores for different years, and link students' scores to teacher effects from multiple years. Recent examples of this approach include the TVAAS layered model, the cross-classified models of Rowan, Correnti, and Miller (2002) and Raudenbush and Bryk (2002), and the persistence model we introduced in McCaffrey et al. (2003).[1]

We provide some specific examples of multivariate longitudinal models. In this section, we give simple versions of the model; more details can be found in McCaffrey et al. (2003) and the references cited below. Across the models, for time t, we let y_{it} denote the student's score, m_t denote the mean score for the relevant population, T_t the student's teacher, and e_{it} the residual error term. To be concrete, we present models for three years of data and for a single subject (e.g., math or reading) and a single cohort of students.

The cross-classified model assumes that student achievement is growing linearly over time and the parameters of this growth trend are student dependent. In other words, a student's growth is given by $m_i + b_i t$. Teacher effects are permanent deflections from this trend line (Raudenbush and Bryk, 2002). For three years of testing, the model is given by

$$y_{i1} = m_i + b_i + T_1 + e_{i1}$$
$$y_{i2} = m_i + 2b_i + T_1 + T_2 + e_{i2} \tag{4.3}$$
$$y_{i3} = m_i + 3b_i + T_1 + T_2 + T_3 + e_{i3} \ .$$

The student-specific intercepts and slopes, m_i and b_i, are assumed to be Gaussian (normally distributed) random variables that are independent across students, with means m and b, variances v_m and v_b, and covariance v_{mb}, all of which are unknown and estimated from the data using maximum likelihood methods. The random intercepts and slopes are also assumed to be independent of the Gaussian residual error terms, the e_{it}'s, which are assumed independent of each other. That is, the random slopes and intercepts are assumed to

---

[1] Some readers might refer to joint modeling as growth modeling. However, because some of the common examples do not provide explicit functional models for growth, we use the term *multivariate modeling*.

fully capture all the student-related influences on scores. Teacher effects are assumed to be mean-zero Gaussian random variables that are independent of all the other variables in the model. Because teacher effects are assumed to have mean zero, they are relative to those of the average teacher for the population.

Because teacher effects are permanent deflections, the effects persist and accumulate in the model for testing at later grades. The model can be extended to include student covariates and nonlinear terms. For example, RCM included a fixed quadratic term in time in the cross-classified model they used to estimate teacher effects (see Chapter Three for details). The cross-classified model is the only model that explicitly models individual growth curves. The other longitudinal models make no explicit assumptions about growth. Instead, they allow the means to vary across test administrations, which implicitly accommodates certain growth models.

TVAAS uses what is called a *layered model* because models for later years of teacher effects build upon the layers from the earlier years. For clarity of presentation, we present a simple version of a layered model, given by

$$
\begin{aligned}
y_{i1} &= m_1 + T_1 + e_{i1} \\
y_{i2} &= m_2 + T_2 + T_1 + e_{i2} \\
y_{i3} &= m_3 + T_3 + T_2 + T_1 + e_{i3}.
\end{aligned}
\tag{4.4}
$$

The key feature of the layered model following the basic TVAAS specification is that the means depend only on time and the school district—the model does not include covariates or school effects. Teacher effects are relative to average teachers in the school district. Teachers affect student achievement when students are in their classes, and this effect persists undiminished at all future years of testing. Teacher effects are independent Gaussian random variables and independent of the residual errors. The residual error terms have mean zero; variances that can differ across time points and pairwise covariances are unrestricted—the covariance for each pair of time points has a separate parameter.[2] All the variance and covariance parameters are estimated from the data using maximum likelihood methods. The complex correlation among the residual errors of the repeated measures of students is meant to provide a means of accounting for student-specific effects on scores and is used in place of covariates for students. The TVAAS specification used by Tennessee to produce teacher effects jointly models scores for five subjects and multiple cohorts. Sanders, Saxton, and Horn (1997) and Ballou, Sanders, and Wright (2003) provide details on the TVAAS layered model.

In McCaffrey et al. (2003), we suggest an alternative to the layered model that allows for the estimation of the strength of the persistence of teacher effects in later years. The model is given by

$$y_{i1} = m_2 + T_1 + e_{i1}$$
$$y_{i2} = m_2 + T_2 + a_{21}T_1 + e_{i2} \qquad (4.5)$$
$$y_{i3} = m_3 + T_3 + a_{32}T_2 + a_{31}T_1 + e_{i3} \ .$$

The parameters, a_{21}, $_{32}$, and a_{31} determine the persistence of prior year teacher effects on current year scores. We call this the *persistence model* because it models the persistence of teacher effects. (Interpretation of the a's is discussed later in the section on modeling prior-year teacher effects.) As with the layered model, the variance of the residual errors is allowed to change across years and the correlations between errors terms are unspecified and estimated from the data. Model parameters are estimated using maximum likelihood methods. We suggest extending the model to include covariates and to model school effects.

Because of disparate assumptions made by the three approaches (covariate adjustment, gain score, and multivariate models), the approaches have different strengths and weaknesses. We briefly discuss these features below, and conclude with some general recommendations.

---

[2] Variance and covariance parameters are constrained so the covariance matrix is positive definite.

Covariate Adjustment Models. Because it subdivides the modeling of the vector of scores into parts where students are fully nested in classrooms, the covariate adjustment model is simple to specify and fit using any standard statistical software package for linear mixed models. It has an additional intuitive appeal because it can be interpreted as all students starting at the same initial level of achievement. However, the estimates will be sensitive to the year chosen as the starting value (see Bryk and Weisberg [1977] and Rogosa and Willett [1982]). In addition, the regression function $E(y_t|y_{t-1})$ can be thought of as predicting the student's achievement with the average teacher (see Chapter Two), as opposed to his or her actual teacher, even if test scores from successive years are not on a single developmental scale. One of the greatest strengths of the covariate adjustment approach is its ability to be extended naturally, via higher-order polynomial terms, to models where scores from successive years are nonlinearly related (although, as noted in Rogosa and Willett [1982], the form of the nonlinear models will be sensitive to the year of testing).

The primary disadvantage of the covariate adjustment model is that fitting the models separately for each year of data ignores important information. It ignores information about student performance in other years that can account for individual student factors and reduce the sampling error and possibly the bias in the estimate of the current-year teacher effect. It also ignores the fact that scores from the future hold information about teachers in the past. Ignoring this information results in what statisticians call inefficient estimates, implying that an alternative technique (e.g., jointly modeling the multiple years of data) could yield estimates with less sampling error. Inefficient estimates will result in larger errors in estimated teacher effects and make inferences about teachers more difficult than efficient estimates will.

If the residual error terms in model 4.1 were independent across years, then the estimates would be efficient. But this holds only under restrictive (and thus unrealistic) conditions for the persistence of teacher effects across years, the functional form for growth in achievement, and the covariance among a student's scores.

Measurement error in test scores can also be problematic for estimating teacher effects with the covariate model. Although test scores are fallible measures of achievement, analysts applying a covariate-adjustment model to estimate teacher effects implicitly or explicitly assume error-free measurement of prior achievement. When measurement error in the prior-year scores is ignored, estimates of the model coefficients are biased. Analytic results suggest that if students are randomly assigned to classes and the distributions of the error-free values of students' prior-year achievement are similar across classes, measurement error will not result in any systematic errors in teacher effects. However, analysts usually assume that students are not randomly assigned and that the distribution of prior achievement does vary across classes. In this case, when distributions of the error-free values of prior achievement differ across classes, measurement error can result in systematic errors in teacher effects. Measurement error can be thought of as creating an omitted covariate; our discussion on the effects of omitting covariates from the model describes a situation in which measurement error is likely to result in bias in teacher effects.[3]

A third disadvantage to covariate models is that students missing either the prior-year or current-year test scores are excluded. Discarding partial data is again inefficient. Furthermore, if students who are missing scores differ systematically from other students, the estimates can be biased (see our discussion on missing data for details). Specialized methods, such as imputation or weighting, are required to avoid bias and use all the available data.

---

[3] As noted by many authors, estimates of treatment effects from observational studies are very sensitive to the assumption that the coefficient on y_{t-1} is constant across all students and treatment and control groups. We suspect that similar sensitivity would occur for estimating teacher effects for observational data with VAM. We are unaware of any direct studies of the sensitivity of teacher effects to the assumption of a constant effect for prior achievement, but we expect that bias would result. However, all the alternative models also assume constant teacher effects across students, so it is not clear whether any of the alternatives would provide better estimates of the teachers' average effects if effects are not constant and students differ across classes.

Gain Score Models. Like the covariate adjustment model, the gain score model is easily specified and fit using standard software. Furthermore, gain score modeling completely accounts for factors that affect only students' levels of achievement. Covariate adjustment models do not necessarily completely remove such factors. On the other hand, as with covariate models, the gain score model, by treating pairs of gains on the same student as independent, is discarding potentially valuable information about individual students that could improve efficiency. In addition, the gain-score approach models growth, and growth is confounded with changes in the test when the scale of the test changes across years. Thus, it is difficult to interpret gain score models for measurements that are not on a single developmental scale. Finally, the gain score model shares two of the potential limitations of the covariate adjustment model: Special methods are required to accommodate partial records, and the model is consistent with only a single assumption about the persistence of teacher effects (namely, that teacher effects on student-level scores persist indefinitely and undiminished).

Multivariate Models. By dealing with the joint distribution of the student outcomes, multivariate models afford a number of advantages. Within the class of linear models, the models are exceedingly flexible, allowing the specification and estimation of a large class of submodels. Indeed, under certain assumptions (see McCaffrey et al. 2003), the covariate adjustment and gain scores models can be viewed as special cases of the multivariate model specified in 4.4. The models allow analysts to explore a variety of assumptions about the persistence of teacher effects as well as the residual covariance of student outcomes. By explicitly modeling the latter, the models efficiently use the available data, and exploiting the residual covariance also makes the models robust to omitted variables in some circumstances (McCaffrey et al. 2003). The models easily accommodate partial student records, and under certain assumptions (see the section "The Effects of Incomplete Records") this provides a further avenue for increased efficiency and less bias in estimates. Finally, while multivariate models such as the layered model and the cross-classified model are interpretable only when scores are on a single developmental scale, the more general specification of the multivariate model provided by McCaffrey et al. (2003) removes that restriction for linearly related scales.

The primary disadvantage of the multivariate models is extreme computational burden. Only certain special cases can be specified easily using standard publicly available linear mixed model packages, and even when models can be specified, in most cases they can be fit only to modestly-sized data sets. While progress is being made to overcome these computational challenges (Rasbash and Goldstein, 1994; DebRoy and Bates, 2003), widely available and flexible solutions are still lacking.

Specification of Teacher Effects as Fixed or Random

Summary: Statistical models can specify teacher effects as "fixed effects," which assume that the observed teachers are the only teachers of interest, or "random effects," which assume that the observed teachers are a sample from a larger population of teachers of interest. The two methods will tend to yield similar conclusions about the variability of teachers but will provide different estimates of individual teacher effects. The differences result from different strategies of the methods for dealing with inherent sampling error of estimated effects.

Statistical models for repeated measures on a single unit, such as multiple students in a classroom or multiple teachers in a district, can treat those units as either fixed or random (Searle, Casella, and McCulloch, 1992).[4] If the units are treated as fixed, then the observed units are assumed to be the only units of interest. Random effects assume that the units are drawn from a larger population of

---

[4] We use the term *fixed teacher effects* to denote the model where the population of teachers is assumed to be fixed, all teachers in the population are in the sample, and a constant effect is associated with each teacher. The models are often characterized by including indicator or dummy variables for each teacher in the regression model for estimating effects. The term is also used in other ways—in ANOVA, to refer to all models in which one does not generalize past the levels of factors included in the model and in multi-level modeling, to refer to models in which coefficients are fixed. We do not use fixed effects in those senses.

similar but unobserved units and that variability among the observed units describes variability in the population. In VAM applications for estimating teacher effects, the primary design choice is whether to model teacher effects as fixed or random. The choice might depend on the particular VAM application. For example, random effects are the natural approach when variance components are of primary interest. Alternatively, in a model fit to data for the specific intention of making inferences about a particular set of teachers (e.g., as might be the case in an accountability setting), fixed effects might be preferable. Early VAM applications (for instance, Murnane, 1975, and Hanushek, 1972) primarily used fixed effects, while more recent applications (including the TVAAS layered model) have used random effects almost exclusively.

For some inferences, the choice between fixed or random effects models will not be of much consequence. For example, although models with fixed teacher effects do not provide the direct estimates of the variance among teachers in effectiveness that random effects models supply, the traditional R^2 from such models can be used to make an analogous inference (i.e., the percentage of the total variability in the outcomes explained by the teachers). Similarly, both approaches provide tests of the null hypothesis that all teacher effects are equal.

However, for other inferences, the choice between fixed and random effects may have important statistical ramifications. Assuming fixed effects results in estimated teacher effects that depend only on the teacher's students, possibly adjusted for the students' characteristics and correlation between scores (or gains) from other years depending on the exact model used. In contrast, when effects are treated as random, the effects are estimated by what are known as best linear unbiased predictors (BLUPs, or, more precisely, estimated best linear predictors, EBLUPs, because estimated variance components are used in calculating the BLUPs) or empirical Bayes estimators (Raudenbush and Bryk, 2002).[5] The key feature of these estimators is

---

[5] Fully Bayesian analyses are possible but have not been used to this point, so we focus on non-Bayesian methods.

that they use data from all teachers to estimate each teacher's effect. This is accomplished by what is known as "shrinking." For very simple models, the estimated teacher effect is given by

$$\hat{\theta}_i = \lambda_i(\bar{y}_i - \bar{y})$$

where $\bar{y}_i$ denotes the average outcome for the teacher's own students and $\bar{y}$ denotes the average outcome for all students. The weight λ_i is less than 1 so the deviation between the classroom mean and total sample means is "shrunk" back toward zero. The BLUP downweights the deviation from the average classroom. The fixed-effect estimate equals the deviation not shrunken toward zero.[6] The amount of shrinking depends on the precision of the teacher's classroom mean and the overall variability among teachers. Greater precision in classroom means and greater variation among teachers both result in less shrinking (Robinson, 1991). In more-complex models, the deviations account for covariates in the model and other sources of correlation. But the basic structure remains: Random-effects models involve shrinking deviations toward zero.

Estimating teacher effects with a random-effects model has both advantages and disadvantages. One advantage is that shrinking reduces the variance of an estimate of an individual teacher effect relative to the fixed-effect estimate. In addition, random effects facilitate modeling prior-year teacher effects by allowing those effects to persist at some level into the future. (See for example, the descriptions of the general model, the layered model, and the cross-classified models in McCaffrey et al. [2003].) Fixed effects could also be modeled across time, but such a model is less straightforward.

The downside of random-effects models is that by shrinking estimates toward the overall mean, random effects force estimated teacher effects to deviate from the true unobserved effects; i.e., they introduce bias. In particular, if the teacher's class is small or the preci-

---

[6] When classes have differing numbers of students, the random effects estimator uses a weighted mean of classroom means rather than the overall average, $\bar{y}$. In such cases, fixed effects analyses still use $\bar{y}$. However, the heuristic notion remains: Random effects shrink deviations back toward zero and fixed effects do not.

sion of the average measure for the class is small (where the measure might be a residual after adjusting for covariates in the model), the shrunken estimate can be far below the teacher's true effect for highly effective teachers and far above the teacher's true effect for extremely ineffective teachers. Although shrunken estimates minimize the average across teachers of the squared error between estimated and true effects (Carlin and Louis, 2000; Raudenbush and Bryk, 2002), they do not provide optimal estimates for individual teachers. In particular, for a teacher whose effect is far from the mean, less shrinkage might provide an estimate with smaller expected squared errors, where expectation is over the possible classes of students the teacher might have taught (Carlin and Louis, 2000). The large deviations between estimated and true effects for the individual teacher might be unacceptable for some inferences. For example, if accountability decisions are made on the basis of a teacher's effect being extreme in the distribution, teachers with small classes will tend to be excluded from accountability actions.

Random-effects modeling also requires specification of the distribution of random effects. All VAM applications we examined assumed Gaussian (normally) distributed random effects. The amount of shrinking will depend on this distributional assumption. There is little theory for selecting the distribution, and the empirical evaluation of the distribution is difficult. Nonparametric techniques and Bayesian techniques relax the assumption for specifying the distribution (see Carlin and Louis, 2000); however, they have not been considered in VAM applications and should be explored in future research. Specification of the distribution of teacher effects is further complicated when data from multiple cohorts or subjects are modeled jointly because such modeling requires specifying the joint distribution of the multiple effects for any individual teacher. One might also model the correlations among effects for teachers in the same school.

Because fixed effects do not shrink estimates toward the mean, the deviations between the estimated effects and true effects will not necessarily be systematically related to the teacher's true effect. Fixed-effect estimates will not necessarily move teachers toward the middle of the distribution in the same manner as BLUPs do, and deviations for individual teachers can be large due to variability in student scores. Moreover, estimated effects for teachers with small classes will tend to be more variable than estimates for teachers with larger classes. Thus, fixed-effect estimates for teachers with small classes will be more likely to be in the extremes of the distribution. Decisions based on teachers being in the extreme of the distribution may be applied more often to teachers with small classes and in a possibly erratic fashion because extreme values will be driven in part by random fluctuations in scores.

Thus, neither a fixed-effects model nor a random-effects model is unambiguously better. The statistical implications of the choice may influence the decision, but it is also partly substantive: The best decision may depend on the particular inferences that are considered most important. If the interest is in estimating the variability of teachers or determining which teacher characteristics correlate with scores, then random effects are likely to be preferable. If the interest is in estimating individual teacher effects, then the choice is less clear. Random-effects models are preferred when estimates that shrink teachers toward the mean—possibly underestimating the most and least effective teachers—are less detrimental to the inference of interest than estimates with large but unsystematic errors. Fixed-effects models are preferred otherwise. When considering the expected squared error in the estimated effect for a randomly chosen teacher or an average across teachers, random-effects estimates find an optimal balance between systematic and random errors. For individual teachers, especially those who deviate substantially from the mean, the random-effects estimate could be undesirable with large squared error. Unfortunately, analysts do not know true teacher effects and therefore do not know which teacher effects should receive less shrinking. Alternative methods such as those proposed by Stern and Cressie (1999), which provide better estimates for teachers with extreme effects, warrant future research. Alternatively, sensitivity analyses that explore the possible errors from using random or fixed effects should be conducted on each individual teacher's estimated effect before decisions are based on that effect. In addition, when making the choice between the two models, one should consider trade-offs between the benefits of shrinkage or fixed-effects estimates in the context of the models' robustness for modeling student covariates because, as discussed below, omitted covariates differentially affect the estimates from the two models.

Omitted Variables, Confounders, and Missing Data

VAM uses data collected in an observational setting (as opposed to an experimental setting). Different schools serve different student populations, teachers make choices about which districts and/or schools in which to teach, and districts and/or schools make choices about which teachers they want to hire. Within schools, principals and teachers may make judgments about which teachers are best suited to teach which students. These factors make the assignment of teachers to students nonrandom and create challenges for estimating teacher effects. Furthermore, the data collected from this observational setting are subject to a number of problems.

In particular, two types of problems arising from these circumstances can distort VAM estimates of teacher effects. First, influences on student learning that are incorrectly modeled or are not modeled at all can be confounded or confused with teacher effects. An example would be a model that does not properly distinguish the effects of teachers from other effects of the school in which the teacher works. The second type of problem is incomplete data. In the case of VAM, two types of incompleteness arise frequently: incomplete data for individual students over time, and incomplete information on the linking of students to teachers. In the following sections, we discuss these problems in detail, beginning with influences that are incorrectly modeled and ending with missing data.

Is the Inclusion of Student Background Variables as Covariates Important?

Summary: The importance of modeling the effects of student background variables depends in a relatively complicated fashion on the interaction of several factors. These factors are the distribution across classes and schools of students with different characteristics, the relationship between the characteristics and outcomes, the relationship between the characteristics and true teacher effects, and the type of model used. When students are separated into distinct subpopulations (e.g. schools) based on background characteristics that are related to outcomes, the potential for bias in estimated teacher effects exists. Under some circumstances, this bias can be mitigated, but in other cases current methods are not capable of removing bias.

Educators, researchers, and policymakers all generally agree that schooling is only one of many factors that affect student achievement and learning (Wang, Haertel, and Walberg, 1993). For example, the ability and aptitude of individual students contribute to their achievement. It has long been recognized that numerous family background characteristics, such as income, parental education, and ethnicity, are strong predictors of student performance. Peer and neighborhood effects often are cited as an influence on student achievement. While there is substantial disagreement about the mechanisms underlying these relationships—for example, whether being raised in a single-parent family influences achievement directly or indirectly through its effect on family income (e.g., McLanahan, 1997)—it is clear that the associations are large. While the relationships between background characteristics and achievement levels are well accepted, less is known about correlates of gains or growth that are the measures used explicitly or implicitly by VAM models. However, there are some data showing that background characteristics predict gains for some populations (Shkolnick et al., 2002).

These various influences on gains or growth could be confounded with and therefore bias estimates of teacher effects, and the question of whether it is necessary to include these variables in the model has been an important point of debate in the VAM literature. Incomplete modeling of additional influences on outcome measures has long been recognized as one of the fundamental threats to causal inferences from non-experimental models. We have encountered a common misperception among analysts and users of VAM results that because TVAAS does not include covariates, student characteristics do not need to be modeled for any VAM applications using longitudinal models. However, this assertion is not necessarily true. Rather, the importance of modeling background variables depends in a relatively complicated fashion on the interaction of several factors. These factors are the distribution across classes and schools of students with different characteristics, the relationship between the characteristics and outcomes, the relationship between the characteristics and true teacher effects, and the type of model used. Therefore, the importance of modeling student background characteristics when using VAM to estimate teacher effects remains an empirical question that must be addressed by each analyst in the context of these specific factors. In this section, we first describe in detail each of the factors influencing the potential for bias. We then discuss which combinations of these factors are most likely to introduce bias into estimated teacher effects.

We begin with the distribution of students with different characteristics because this factor determines whether the other factors can create bias. If classes are balanced on omitted background variables (i.e., the distribution of the background variables is the same for all classes), then the omitted variables have only the effect of increasing residual (unexplained) variance. They do not result in any bias. Therefore, we do not consider this case further, and turn our attention to the more realistic case in which the distribution of the omitted variables varies across classes or schools. We refer to this as "clustering" of the omitted variable. For example, average family income, which is excluded from many VAM models, tends to vary considerably among schools, and greater income is strongly related to achievement. This clustering is not limited to classes but can occur at the school level as well—even in longitudinal studies—because students with differing characteristics might never attend the same schools. For example, low-income students and high-income students might attend completely different groups of schools (maybe in different districts) with no transfer among these schools. Thus, the population of students is stratified into distinct subpopulations that differ on the average values of variables that are not included in the model. This stratification of students into subpopulations that do not mix on the basis of variables not included in the model will bias estimated teacher effects, even with complex models such as the layered or cross-classified models. (See McCaffrey et al. [2003] for details.) Whether it is possible to remove this bias by the inclusion of the variables depends on the other factors that we discuss below.

The first of these factors is the relationship between student characteristics and outcomes. The critical distinction is between that of an individual effect and a "contextual" or "compositional" effect (Raudenbush and Bryk, 2002). An individual effect refers to a characteristic of an individual student that is related to outcomes; for example, one might observe that students participating in free and reduced price lunch programs tend to make smaller gains. Alternatively, a contextual effect refers to aggregate characteristics of schools or classes that are related to outcomes. For example, one might observe that students in schools with a high percentage of students participating in free and reduced price lunch programs tend to make smaller gains, and this may be true even for students who do not participate. A more formal distinction between the two kinds of effects in the context of linear regression models is as follows: Suppose that student j in school i has characteristic x_{ij}, and let x_i equal the school-level mean of these student characteristics. A contextual effect exists when the relationship between the characteristics and outcomes is of the form $Bx_{ij} = B(x_{ij} - x_i) + Bx_i$ with $B \neq C$. Models that include the only term Bx_{ij} implicitly assume that no contextual effects exist because $Bx_{ij} = B(x_{ij} - x_i) + Bx_i$. Below, we discuss issues with controlling for student characteristics when contextual effects exist. The discussion applies to other school- or classroom-level predictors such as district policies or school governance.

The second factor is the relationship between student characteristics and true teacher effectiveness. Because teachers are not randomly assigned to schools, there is the possibility that true teacher effects can be correlated with aggregate student characteristics. Teachers of different levels of effectiveness may select or be selected by schools serving different student populations. For example, schools serving at-risk students are often found to have a greater proportion of novice teachers and teachers lacking full teaching credentials (Shkolnick et al., 2002).

The final factor determining the impact of omitted background variables on estimated teacher effects in the presence of stratification is whether teacher effects are estimated with either fixed- or random-effects models. We first discuss the impact of omitted student-level covariates ignoring classroom- or school-level variables and contextual effects. We then turn to adjusting for classroom- or school-level variables and contextual effects. As we discuss below, methods exist for accounting for student-level variables when contextual effects are not present, but no good methods currently exist to adjust for aggregate-level variables like contextual effects.

Student-Level Variables. In the case of fixed-effects models, confounding can in principle be addressed by including the appropriate background variables, in the appropriate manner, as covariates in the model.[7] Fixed-effects models can remove confounding without introducing bias regardless of whether or not student-level background variables are correlated with teacher effects.[8] Of course, including the appropriate variables in the appropriate manner is often difficult, and the adequacy of these covariate adjustments is often a point of debate. Variables that are omitted because they are not available (e.g., parental education) continue to confound estimated teacher effects. Moreover, if confounding is to be fully removed, the functional form of the variables must be correct, and the variables should be measured with little error. Despite these caveats, direct inclusion of available

---

[7] Recall that we are using *fixed effects* to indicate that the population of teachers is fixed and all teachers are represented, in effect, by a dummy variable.

[8] Correlation between teachers and student characteristics could occur because teachers are generally less effective with certain types of students—for example, teachers might be less effective at teaching students who do not speak English. If this is true, covariate adjustment for the characteristics associated with less-effective teaching will remove difference in scores due to less-effective teaching. This might be justified because as a group students with such characteristics score lower. Therefore analysts might consider low scores to be function of the students, not the individual teachers. However, such an analysis might mask the difficulty of teaching such students and provide an inaccurate estimate of teacher effects. In this case, the problem is one of defining a teacher effect: If all teachers are less effective with certain groups, is this a teacher effect or a group effect? The definition will depend on the inference, and the modeling approach will need to be consistent with the chosen definition.

variables as covariates in the model would be a natural choice to reduce confounding for fixed-effects models.

The situation for random-effects models is more complex. The
statistical models assume that the random teacher effects are independent of covariates. Because of this assumption, the estimation
procedure for random-effects models attributes to the covariate the
true effect of the covariate *and* the portion of the teacher effect that
co-varies with the student characteristics. The teacher-effect estimates
receive only the residual portion of the true effect that is uncorrelated
with the covariate. The estimation procedure exaggerates the estimated effects of the characteristics and understates the effects of
teachers. The model "overcorrects" for the covariate at the expense of
the teacher effect, resulting in bias in parameter values (including
variance components) and the estimated teacher effects. For example,
if teachers with large positive true effects are teaching proportionately
more students from high-income families and we adjust for income,
the model will underestimate the teachers' effectiveness. The amount
of bias depends on several factors, including the strength of correlation between true effects and covariates and between covariates and
scores.

Thus, analysts cannot add covariates to the model and assume
that the resulting teacher effects are unbiased. If true teacher effects
were uncorrelated with the covariates, then adding covariate would
produce unbiased effects (assuming the specification of the covariates
is correct). However, if true teacher effects were correlated with the
covariates, then adding covariate would produce biased effects. But
excluding covariates will also create bias in estimated effects.[9] For

---

[9] Analysts can use a Hausman specification test to test for correlation between the covariates
and the unobserved random effects (Greene, 1997). This tests the null hypothesis of no correlation between covariates and unobserved random teacher effects. If the test rejects the null
hypothesis, then analysts cannot just include covariates in the model without incurring bias
in estimated teacher effects. If the test fails to reject the null, then analysts might consider
adding covariates to the model. However, failure to reject the null is not evidence that it is
true. Failure to reject the null hypothesis might also occur if the analysis lacks statistical
power to detect the correlation. Specification tests typically have limited power to detect
effects, so adding covariates after failing to reject the null is typically unadvisable and specification tests have limited value.

student-level covariates without contextual effects, this conundrum can be overcome using methods suggested by Ballou, Sanders, and Wright (2003). They suggest regressing scores (gains in scores, to be precise) on covariates while treating teachers as fixed. For reasons discussed earlier, the estimated coefficients are unbiased. Next, scores are adjusted by predictions based on the unbiased coefficient estimates.[10] Finally, the random effects model is fit using the adjusted scores. Again, provided the covariate specification is correct, the estimated teacher effect would be unbiased by student level covariates.

Classroom-Level Variables and Contextual Effects. By treating teachers as fixed effects and including covariates or by using the Ballou, Sanders, and Wright (2003) method with random-effects models, analysts can control for student-level variables. However, we know of no current method to disentangle true teacher effects from student background characteristics in the presence of classroom-level variables and contextual effects and correlation between true teacher effects and student characteristics.

Fixed-effects models attribute all classroom-level effects to teachers. Because the fixed effects account for all the variability among classrooms, the model cannot include any classroom-level variables other than teachers and the mean. Thus, with fixed-effects models, no direct method exists to adjust for classroom-level variables or contextual effects.[11] For random effects, the methods of Ballou, Sanders, and Wright (2003) have limited value for classroom-level variables and contextual effects because their method uses within-classroom variability to estimate the coefficients. Aggregate-level variables have no within-classroom variability. Although extensions exist, they require additional assumptions and data on teachers who change schools, which are often unavailable. Furthermore, these extensions did not perform well even with the very large TVAAS application

---

[10] If the covariates are denoted by the vector x and the estimated coefficients are denoted by the vector b then the prediction is $u = x'b$ and the adjusted score is $r = y - u$.

[11] For sensitivity analysis with fixed effects models, the analyst might first regress scores or gain scores on classroom-level variables; aggregate student-level variable effects and obtain the residuals; then use these residuals to estimate fixed-effects models. This procedure overadjusts for the covariates but might be useful for sensitivity analyses.

considered by Ballou, Sanders, and Wright (2003). Sensitivity analyses that repeat the estimation with and without classroom-level variables and aggregated student-level variables appear to be the best option at present.

When faced with the challenge of controlling for covariates, TVAAS chose to exclude student covariates rather than possibly underestimate teacher effects. The Dallas accountability system made the opposite choice when deciding on a model for estimating teacher effects. As discussed in Chapter Three, that system uses a complex covariate-adjustment model that includes many student background variables, such as race and language proficiency, at the individual level and aggregated to the school level. Details are found in Webster and Mendro (1997). Thus, one team chose to err on the side of possibly confounding effects and the other chose to err on the side of possibly overcorrecting.

The problems we have discussed suggest the bias that will occur when specific conditions hold—for instance, when omitted variables that predict gains cluster across distinct subpopulations of students attending different schools. Whether such conditions hold is an empirical question. For example, an examination by Ballou, Sanders, and Wright (2003) of data from Tennessee and the TVAAS layered model finds that omitting student-level free and reduced lunch status does not appear to greatly influence estimated teacher effects when comparing the traditional TVAAS estimates to those that use their proposed alternative method. However, they do find evidence that controlling for contextual effects might have greater effects on their estimating, suggesting the contextual effect could be resulting in systematic error when they are omitted from the model. In McCaffrey et al. (2003), we find similar empirical results in a limited example (see the section entitled "Sampling Error" for details on this example).

Disentangling School and District Effects from the Effects of Teachers
Summary: In estimating teacher effects with VAM, the possibility of school or district effects on student achievement must be considered. If such effects are omitted from models, they are implicitly subsumed

by teacher effects, which may bias what analysts conceive to be true teacher effects. Alternatively, if they are included in models and teachers of differential effectiveness cluster at the school or district level, part of true teacher effects will be attributed to schools or districts. Analysts must decide which potential error is more acceptable.

Teachers may or may not be the most important input to student achievement within the formal educational system, but they clearly are not the only one. Other inputs at the school and district level may exert appreciable influence as well. For example, a school or district may influence achievement by providing extracurricular activities, by establishing policies for evaluating student work, and by less direct means of influencing the peer group's attitudes toward achievement. It is not clear how large the independent contributions of schools and districts are, and these contributions undoubtedly vary markedly in size from place to place. Nonetheless, analyses that attempt to estimate the effects of teachers need to be able to distinguish teacher effects from the effects of the schools and districts within which they are nested. Here we discuss only school effects, but the same logic would apply to other levels of nesting.

Simply omitting school effects from the model (as is often done in recent VAM studies, as well as in the TVAAS layered model) results in mistakenly attributing these effects to teachers. These school effects include context and direct and indirect school effects. It is not entirely clear what share of context and indirect school effects are properly considered teacher effects. As discussed in Chapter Two, to the extent that teacher effects depend on the school context or indirect school effects, some inferences require the context effect and indirect school effects as part of the teacher effect. Other inferences—for example, evaluating the teacher's effectiveness for the purpose of staffing schools—require separating these sources. Thus, the impact of excluding school effects from models when context or indirect effects exist will depend on the desired inference and whether or not these effects should be distinguished from teacher effects. But because context and indirect effect are completely confounded with teacher effects, the two can be separated only by untested assumptions, such as an assumption that teacher effects are constant over time.

Regardless of whether context and indirect effects are part of the teacher effect, it is clear that direct school effects—the effects that the school has on students regardless of the teachers in the building—should not be considered part of the teacher effect. Thus, excluding schools from the model when these direct effects exist will result in biased estimates of teacher effects, whereas including school fixed effects in the model will remove this bias. An additional advantage of including school fixed effects is that student characteristics that cluster at the school level will not be confounded with teacher effects, because the effects of the clustered student characteristics will be attributed to the school.

Unfortunately, modeling school effects, like modeling covariates, is not as simple as adding school fixed effects to remove all the bias. Empirically distinguishing teacher effects from school effects is difficult even if context and indirect effects do not exist. If teachers of varying effectiveness cluster by school, then teacher effects will be confounded with school effects because typically we cannot track teachers across schools. Any model that attempts to estimate school effects will most likely attribute some of the teacher effects to schools. For example, a model with fixed effects for schools will completely attribute to the school the difference between the average effect of teachers in the school and the system-wide average teacher effect. All teacher effects will be determined relative to other teachers in the same school. This is because the estimation process essentially first removes the school effects and then estimates all teacher effects relative to the schools. For models with random school and random teacher effects the estimation process does not remove school effects and estimates teacher effect relative to schools. However, the estimation process will tend to assign variability at the school level to the school effects, regardless of the sources of the variability. So even with random school and teacher-effects models, context, direct, and indirect school effects and heterogeneity of true teacher effects across schools will all be associated with schools rather than teachers.[12]

To date, there has been little empirical exploration of the size of school effects and the sensitivity of teacher effects to modeling of school effects. However, in McCaffrey et al. (2003) we found—with a very small heterogeneous sample of schools—that including school fixed effects greatly changed the inferences about teacher effectiveness. (Additional details on the example are in the section below entitled "Sampling Error.") It is unclear whether this difference was the result of removing school effects or effects of the heterogeneous grouping among schools of students with different backgrounds. Results from this small study should not be taken as evidence of the importance of schools, but they do suggest that including school fixed effects can change inferences about teachers in some settings and analyses should check for the sensitivity of results to the inclusion of school effects.

Disentangling the Effects of Earlier Teachers and Schools from Estimated Teacher Effects

Summary: Because VAM follows students over time, typically linked to multiple teachers, analysts must develop models for the effects of prior teachers on current scores. The different modeling approaches (covariate adjustment, gain score, longitudinal) make different assumptions about how teacher effects accumulate. Gain score models assume that prior teachers have no effects on current year growth. All currently used multivariate models (layered and cross-classified) assume that teacher effects persist undiminished into the future. It is possible to generalize the multivariate models to allow teacher effects to affect future outcomes differently from current outcomes.

Underlying VAM is the notion that student learning is cumulative, and that educational entities—specifically teachers, schools, and

---

[12] The exact allocation of school-level variance in the random effects model is complex, but school-level variance—regardless of the source—will generally be attributed to random school effects and not to teacher effects.

school systems—make incremental and lasting inputs to student knowledge. For example, Pederson, Faucher, and Eaton (1978) report on a case study of a teacher who affected student outcomes into adulthood. More generally, the effects of teachers, schools, and school systems from previous years are likely to contribute to students' outcomes in the current year. To avoid confounding, effective model structures for scores or gains in the current year must acknowledge this possibility by accounting for these prior effects. In this section, we focus for concreteness primarily on the effects of prior teachers because the considerations and model accommodations appropriate for prior-teacher effects carry over without change to the effects of prior schools and school systems. We briefly revisit the latter issue at the end of the section.

Studies using either the covariate adjustment or gain score models include only the current-year teacher's effect in the models for the current-year outcome (Rowan, Correnti, and Miller, 2002; Webster and Mendro, 1997; Wright, Horn, and Sanders, 1997). As a result of this assumption and conditioning on prior scores, the covariate adjustment assumes that prior-year teacher effects persist at the same level as student-level characteristics. Gain score models include only the current-year teacher effects, implicitly assuming that prior-year teacher effects do not persist on future gains.

Multivariate models such as the layered model and cross-classified model include the effects of past teachers in addition to that of the current teacher in the model for scores at each year. However, both models assume that teacher effects on level scores (i.e., score for a single year, not a gain score) persist indefinitely into the future without diminishing. As shown in McCaffrey et al. (2003), Sanders, Saxton, and Horn (1997), and Ballou, Sanders, and Wright (2003), and noted previously in this monograph, this assumption results in single-year gain scores that depend only on the current-year teacher. Thus, while these models assume that a teacher has a permanent effect on a student's level of performance, they do so by forcing teachers to have no effects on future growth.

As described previously, the persistence model (4.5) allows teacher effects on level scores to change over time, with the parameters describing the changes to effects being estimated from the data. Furthermore, unlike the layered or cross-classified models, the persistence model results in gains that depend on the prior-year teacher effects. To understand this, consider the model for a student's grade 2 and grade 3 scores. From Equation 4.5 they are given by:

$$y_2 = m_2 + T_2 + a_{21}T_1 + e_2 \tag{4.6}$$

$$y_3 = m_3 + T_3 + a_{32}T_2 + a_{31}T_1 + e_3. \tag{4.7}$$

By subtracting Eq. 4.6 from Eq. 4.7, we obtain the following equation for the gain score:

$$y_3 - y_2 = (m_3 - m_2) + T_3 + (a_{32} - 1)T_2 + (a_{31} - a_{21})T_1 + e_3 - e_2.$$

Thus, gains from grade 2 to grade 3 depend on the second grade teacher through the term $(a_{32} - 1)T_2$ and the first grade teacher through the term $(a_{31} - a_{21})T_1$. With the persistence model of McCaffrey et al. (2003), teacher effects from grades 1 and 2 affect both level scores at grade 3 and gains from grade 2 to grade 3. In particular, when $a_{32} < 1$, if T_2 is positive then the second grade teacher has a negative contribution on gains—and vice versa if T_2 is negative. This is a form of regression to the mean because the effects of the teacher "wear off" over time and the student test scores drift back toward performance that is no longer affected by the second grade teacher. Conversely, when $a_{32} > 1$, if T_2 is positive then the second grade teacher has a positive effect on growth during third grade—and vice versa if T_2 is negative. When a_{32} is greater than one, effective prior teachers accelerate growth and ineffective teachers decelerate growth.[13] Similar results apply to the other a parameters.

---

[13] Simple algebra shows that the covariate adjustment model also implicitly assumes that gain scores will depend on prior teacher effects. Because in most practical settings the coefficient for the prior score in the covariate adjustment model is less than one, a teacher's effect on growth will be the opposite of the effect on levels.

When we applied our persistence model to three years of math score data from students attending a small sample of schools (see McCaffrey et al. [2003]), we estimated that teacher effects dampen very quickly, i.e., the a's were substantially smaller than one. Furthermore, we found that the model that allowed for dampening better fit the data than the layered model, which assumed that effects persisted undiminished. We found, however, that estimated teacher effects are moderately correlated (0.69) between our model and the layered model. Because these results are from one modestly sized example, they should be interpreted not as general trends but rather as an impetus for further exploration of models that make more flexible assumptions about the persistence of teacher effects.

Finally, as noted previously, the assumptions about the nature of the school and school system effects from prior years are the same as those that can be made about prior-year teacher effects. Any approaches used for teachers could be used with other schooling effects. To date, however, longitudinal models have ignored prior-year school effects in models for the current-year scores, implicitly assuming that the effects decay to zero in one year. Covariate adjustment models assume that they persist only as they contribute to prior-year test scores—i.e., their effects decay at the same rate as the effects of all other attributes to prior achievement. There are no empirical explorations of the robustness of estimates to assumptions about prior-year schooling effects. Because the treatment of school effects is likely to have great influence on estimated teacher effects in some populations (see McCaffrey et al., 2003), we expect that estimates will be sensitive to modeling of prior-year schooling effects in some situations as well.

The Effects of Incomplete Records

Summary: Real longitudinal student achievement data will inevitably contain incomplete student achievement records. The accuracy of estimated teacher effects in the presence of incomplete records is sensitive to models for the nature of missing data and to the analytic approach. Excluding incomplete records, as might be common in covariate adjustment or gain scores models, might be particularly susceptible to bias. Longitudinal models can more readily accommodate incomplete records but still make assumptions about the nature of the missing data.

Longitudinal data provide unique and powerful opportunities. However, longitudinal data are difficult to collect and many students will be missing scores for at least one test administration. Students can be missing scores because they transfer into or out of schools or districts included in the scope of tracking for the data system. They can be missing scores because of absence from school or because they skipped a section of testing. Students can also be missing scores because of administrative rules that exclude them from testing. For example, students who lack proficiency in English are often excluded.

The accuracy of estimated teacher effects in the presence of incomplete records is sensitive to models for the nature of missing data and to the analytic approach. Statisticians model the nature of missing data in longitudinal studies using the following classification (Little and Rubin, 2002): missing completely at random, missing at random, and missing not at random.[14]

Data are missing completely at random (MCAR) if for each grade the distribution of the likely values of missing scores equals the distribution of the observed scores after conditioning on any background covariates included in the model. Data are missing at random (MAR) if for each grade the distribution of likely values of missing scores equals the distribution of observed scores conditional on the observed scores at other grades (and background variables). To be specific, consider an example where the data contain scores from two grades and all students have data from the first year of testing but some students are missing scores for the second year of testing. For simplicity, assume that there are no other relevant background characteristics. MCAR implies that the distribution of the unobserved scores at year 2 equals the distribution of the observed scores regardless of the year 1 score. MAR implies that the distribution of the un-

---

[14] Statisticians also use more technical classification of ignorable and nonignorable missing data. Data missing not at random are nonignorable; typically, the data missing completely at random or missing at random are ignorable, See Little and Rubin (2002) for details.

observed scores at year 2 equals the distribution of observed scores conditional on the year 1 score. That is, students with the same year 1 score have the same likely values of scores for year 2, regardless of whether or not the score is observed.

The final classification of missing data is missing not at random (MNAR). Data are MNAR if conditional on the observed scores at other years, the distribution of unobserved scores in a given year differs from the distribution of observed scores in that year. In the previous example, the data are MNAR if a student with missing year 2 scores tends to score lower (or higher) than his/her counterpart with equal year 1 scores and observed year 2 scores. Alternatively, data are MNAR if students with low (or high) scores are more likely to be missing scores.

There are two basic approaches to the analysis of longitudinal data with incomplete records. The first uses only students with complete records, ignoring the partially complete records. The second approach uses all the records, including incomplete records, to estimate teacher effects and model parameters.

Covariate adjustment models that include prior-year scores as covariates typically use only records with both current and prior-year scores observed, although more-sophisticated analyses may use some form of imputation (Schafer, 1998) of missing scores. Models for a single year of gains also generally use only records with the gain score observed. Alternatively, longitudinal models, and specifically the TVAAS layered model, typically use more than two years of scores and include both complete and incomplete records.

Analyses such as covariate models and single-year gain models that include only complete observations will tend to provide valid estimates of teacher effects only when the missing data are MCAR. Models that include both complete and incomplete records typically provide valid estimates of teacher effects when the data are MAR (or by implication MCAR) but not when the data are MNAR.

To date, there has been no systematic study of the nature of missing data in longitudinal test score data for VAM, but we do know that students who miss tests often score lower than students with complete data. This does not necessarily imply the data are

MNAR, because observed scores in incomplete records might account for the differences between students who complete and those who miss a test. Also, the robustness of estimated teacher effects to violations of the implied MAR and MCAR assumptions in most VAM models has not been studied. In some situations, estimates are surprisingly robust to the violation of MAR (Rubin, Stern, and Vehovar, 1995), but these situations are very different from the estimation of teacher effects.

Several approaches are possible for expanding models to better account for missing data. Weighting records can allow models fit with only complete cases to provide accurate estimates when the data are MAR (Robins, Rotnitzky, and Zhao, 1995). There are also several approaches to modeling data with values that are potentially MNAR. Little (1995) suggests jointly modeling the outcomes and indicators for response allowing for common random student effects to be in the model for both outcomes and response. Little (1993) and Hedeker and Gibbons (1997) suggest pattern mixture models in which the data are stratified by response pattern and separate models are fit for each pattern. Parametric models for response have also been proposed (Diggle and Kenward, 1994). Alternatively, sensitivity analyses can be conducted whereby multiple models representing a range of explicit assumptions about differences between the distributions of observed and unobserved scores are fit to the data to yield multiple estimates of teacher effects. Sensitivity to missing data is monitored by the variability in the multiple estimates of each teacher's effects.

Linking Students to Teachers

Summary: For a variety of reasons such as team teaching and transfer, the one-to-one correspondence between student test scores and teachers may be imperfect. Such incomplete linkages should be addressed to avoid confounding the effects of a given teacher with those of other teachers. There are a number of possible modifications that can be made to VAM models to handle these data circumstances.

Teacher effects are estimated by observing the outcomes of their students. Estimation requires that students be linked to their teachers. If all students attended just one school and were taught by only one teacher in each year, then linking students to teachers would be simple provided administrative records (class rosters) were accurately maintained. However, the real world is not so simple. Students change schools in midyear. Teachers also change in midyear. Some teachers team-teach or share responsibility for teaching a subject. Some subjects are not the specific responsibility of any teacher. For example, in middle schools reading is not necessarily taught as an independent subject but as part of most other classes. Each of these scenarios creates imperfect correspondences between students and teachers and must be handled properly to avoid confounding the effects of a particular teacher with those of other teachers.

Many possible modeling assumptions exist for dealing with the complex problem of linking students to teachers. For team teaching, one possible assumption is that both teachers provide equal education to the students or that time in class equals educational inputs. Administrative records can be maintained to identify each teacher's share of inputs to the students, and both teachers can be included in the model for the student's achievement or growth weighted by their contribution to inputs. Similarly, if analysts are willing to assume that every day of schooling represents equal educational inputs, then midyear transfers of teachers or students could be modeled by including multiple weighted teacher effects in the model for each student's outcome with weights equal to the proportion of days in the class.[15] Another assumption is that students who transfer or have team teachers have outcomes that are similar in distribution to other students, so these students can be excluded from the data. Yet another possible

---

[15] Assuming that all days of schooling provide equal educational inputs might be incorrect. For example, Smith (1998) found in a sample of classes from the Chicago public schools that a steep drop in academic work occurred during the last six weeks of the school year and schooling was "reliably and continuously focused on teaching the grade-level curriculum outlined by the district and state" in only 13 weeks of the school year (p. 23). Teachers used the remainder of the weeks for review or other topics not contained in the curriculum.

assumption is that students with complex links have the average teacher and so can be modeled without a link to any teacher.

Several applications of VAM either provide no explicit mention of the methods for modeling students who transfer or otherwise have no links to teachers (Rowan, Correnti, and Miller, 2002; Webster and Mendro, 1997) or exclude students with incomplete data (Rivken, Hanushek, and Kain, 2000; Wright, Horn, and Sanders, 1997; Sanders and Rivers, 1996). In addition, these studies make no comments about team teachers. TVAAS explicitly models team teachers, weighting each teacher's effect by the share of instructional time (Sanders, Saxton, and Horn, 1997). As a simple example, the fifth grade math score for a student who had two teachers in grade 4 for math, each providing half of the instruction, and one teacher in each of grades 3 and 5, is given by:

$$y_5 = m_5 + T_3 + \frac{1}{2} T_{4,A} + \frac{1}{2} T_{4,B} + T_5 + e_5.$$

TVAAS also includes students who transfer in midyear but links them to a teacher only if they are in one classroom for more than 150 days (Ballou, Sanders, and Wright, 2003). Student who do not link to teachers because of transfer or because no teacher has responsibility for teaching them are included in the model estimation with no explicit teacher link; i.e., such students are assumed to have the average teacher.

The likely size of the bias introduced through incorrect linking or unlinked students will depend in part on the number of students who transfer, are team taught, have no teacher, or have some other complex links with teachers. Currently, no empirical investigations of such issues exist in the context of VAM. However, in conversations with educators about VAM, we have found that mobility is always a concern especially for those from urban districts that report high rates of mobility. More generally, research shows that student mobility is widespread. According to data collected through the National Assessment of Educational Progress (NAEP) 1998 Math Assessment, 34 percent of fourth graders, 21 percent of eighth graders, and 10 percent of twelfth graders changed schools at least once in the previous two years (U.S. Department of Education, 2002). One survey of more than 50 local education agencies throughout the United States reveals that in many districts the proportion of students enrolled in a school for less than the entire academic year often exceeds 30–40 percent (Ligon and Paredes, 1992). Also, Title 1 funding has historically supported special classes for low-income students, so that low-income students might be more likely to have multiple teachers.

Issues Arising from the Use of Achievement Tests as an Outcome

Student achievement is measured imperfectly by tests. The timing of tests does not generally conform to the school year, and tests contain measurement error. These errors can differentially affect student scores and estimated teacher effects based on those scores. Alternative scalings and constructions of tests are possible, and there is no objective criterion for choosing among the alternatives. However, inferences about teacher effects are likely to be sensitive to these choices. We examine these issues in the following sections, along with discussions on score inflation and the relationship between the scale of teacher effectiveness and the scale of student achievement.

The Effects of Timing of Tests

Summary: Testing is infrequent (typically only once a year), and the testing interval usually includes portions of two grades and summer recess. Studies have shown that changes in achievement over summer recess are related to student characteristics such as socioeconomic status and ethnicity. However, a small simulation study suggests these differences may be sufficiently small to have little impact on VAM estimates of teacher effects. Changing the timing of tests to fall-spring testing would in theory provide more isolated estimates of teacher effects, but research suggest that fall-spring testing introduces other, perhaps larger, biases than the more common spring-to-spring testing.

Most school testing programs test once during the second half of the school year, and the testing typically occurs at least several weeks before the end of the year. Thus, the test cannot measure the effect of a full year in a teacher's class. In addition, the measured growth between test administrations will involve change during a time interval that includes part of the previous year of schooling as well as summer recess. Inclusion of change during this time period might also distort estimates of a teacher's effect on the student. Of particular concern is the empirical evidence showing that change during the summer recess varies across identifiable groups of students. Both socio-economic status (SES) and ethnicity have been shown in some studies to correlate with changes in achievement during summer break, with minority and low-SES students having the smallest gains (see, e.g., Alexander, Entwisle, and Olson, 2001).

In theory, testing twice a year—very near the beginning and end of the school year—would provide more isolated estimates of teacher effects, but historical evidence suggests that this form of testing may produce other, perhaps even larger, biases. Linn (2000) noted that large-scale evaluations of the Title I program in the 1970s and early 1980s suggested that annual testing provided more accurate estimates of student growth than fall-spring testing, with the latter showing a substantial positive bias in overall estimates of growth. He noted:

> Linn [Dunbar, Harnisch, and Hastings] (1982) reviewed a number of factors that together tended to inflate the estimates of gain in the fall-to-spring testing cycle results. These included such considerations as student selection, scale conversion errors, administration conditions, administration dates compared to norming dates, practice effects, and [score inflation from] teaching to the test (Linn, 2000, p. 5).

Even if annual testing provides more accurate estimates of mean growth, it does potentially bias comparisons among teachers for the reasons noted. Models can account for differential summer gains by controlling for student level covariates likely to be correlated with those gains (i.e., SES and minority status). Models might also explicitly account for the mixing of teacher effects across years. The model of McCaffrey et al. (2003) is one approach to addressing this problem because it allows gains to depend on prior-year teacher effects and estimates how much to downweight those effects. However, the amount of bias due to differential summer trends may be so small that these steps are unnecessary. In a small simulation study, we explored the likely effects of differential summer gains on estimated teacher effects and estimates of the variability among teachers. We found that in longitudinal models, differential summer gains of realistic magnitudes are likely to have only minimal effects on estimates. However, these findings are based on a limited simulation and limited (mostly old) data on trends in scores, so additional investigation may be warranted.

Issues Posed by the Construction and Scaling of Tests
Summary: The scale for measuring achievement is not predetermined by the nature of achievement but is chosen by the test developer. Alternative scalings and constructions of tests are possible, and there is no objective criterion for choosing among these alternatives. Scores from test forms for different grades must be vertically linked to a single scale so that achievement at one grade can be compared to achievement at other grades. Various methods for such linking exist. Changes to the scaling of tests, the weight given to alternative topics, or the methods for vertical linking could change our conclusions about the relative achievement or growth in achievement across classes of students. These changes would influence inferences about teacher effects. While our explorations suggest that estimated variance components might be insensitive to some alternatives, we expect that estimated teacher effects could be very sensitive to changes in scaling or other alterations to test construction and vertical linking of different test forms. There is currently no empirical evidence about the sensitivity of gain scores or teacher effects to such alternatives.

Many of the inferences based on VAM require an interval scale of teacher effectiveness. An *interval scale* (Stevens, 1946, 1968) is one on which any given arithmetic difference has the same substantive meaning at any point on the scale. If a scale is interval, any linear transformation of the scale will also be interval, but any nonlinear transformation will necessarily be non-interval. In practice, no VAM models use direct measures of teacher effectiveness. Rather, they use measures of student achievement and in effect assume (1) that these are on interval scales and (2) that these interval scales of student achievement have a linear mapping onto the latent scale of teacher effectiveness. Initially, we will accept the use of student achievement measures as a proxy for teacher effectiveness and will discuss issues that arise in VAM because of the construction and scaling of these measures. Following this discussion, we address the assumption that student achievement maps linearly onto the latent scale of teacher effectiveness.

One inference that clearly depends on an interval scale is comparisons of the estimated effectiveness of those teachers teaching students who begin the time period in question at substantially different levels of achievement. A nonlinear transformation of the score scale will alter the relative rates of change shown by these two groups of students. Even when students begin at the same point on the scale, however, the interval nature of the scale is important. For example, consider two teachers whose students begin at the same level of performance but show different rates of growth during the year. The apparent size of that difference would be sensitive to nonlinear transformations of scale. Thus, inferences about the relative effectiveness of teachers assume that the scale on which performance is reported is robust and is approximately interval—that is, that departures from a true interval scale are small relative to the differences between teachers.

The issues of scaling raised by VAM are of two types: the general indeterminacy of cross-sectional scales and issues that arise in constructing a vertical or developmental scale—that is, a scale that places performance on the tests administered to successive grades onto a single scale so that growth can be measured across grades or ages. The creation of a vertical scale layers additional issues on top of those that arise in constructing a cross-sectional scale. Therefore, we begin by discussing the indeterminacy of cross-sectional scales before moving to issues of vertical scaling.

Indeterminacy of Cross-Sectional Scales. The general indeterminacy of achievement scales has long been noted in the psychometric literature. Cross-sectional inferences are not sensitive to linear transformations of scale, but nonlinear transformations are problematic. Spencer (1983) and others have noted that many of the scales that can be seen as reasonable representations of performance on achievement tests are nonlinear transformations of each other and therefore can provide substantially different conclusions about differences and trends. Spencer noted that even some of the most basic conclusions about student performance, such as the ranking of group means, are not necessarily invariant under nonlinear transformations of score scales. Specifically, rankings of means are necessarily invariant under monotonic, nonlinear transformations of scale only if the distribution functions of the two scales are stochastically ordered—that is, only if for all numbers x, $F(x) \leq G(x)$, where F and G are the scaling functions (Spencer, 1983). In other words, rankings of means are necessarily invariant only if the cumulative distribution functions of the two scales do not cross. More important for present purposes is the fact that even when the distribution functions are stochastically ordered and the ordering of means is therefore preserved by a scale transformation, other patterns upon which important inferences are based—including some of the important inferences based on VAM—may not be robust under nonlinear transformations of scale.

This problem could be circumvented if there were a clear reason to choose one scale from those available, but when measuring student achievement, we usually lack an unambiguous basis for selecting among them. In this respect, psychometrics is unlike measurement in many other areas. In physics, for example, the acceptance of certain laws pertaining to the behavior of gases allows one to deduce that certain measures, such as the common scales of temperature, constitute interval scales. In contrast, there are no such laws specifying the relationships between achievement and other variables. In addition, there is often no generally accepted basis for assuming any given distribution of the latent trait, which eliminates another potential basis for choosing among scales.

For our purposes, however, we are interested not in the theoretical indeterminacy of achievement scales but rather in their practical effects on the robustness of inferences based on the scales used. For many uses, the indeterminacy of scale may not have a major impact. While the range of possible scales is theoretically unlimited, only a few are widely used in modern measurement of achievement, and the cross-sectional relationships among these few are typically very strong. Thus, Hoover (1984a) noted that the purportedly interval developmental standard scores of some test publishers have nearly perfect cross-sectional correlation with the grade equivalent scale, which is expected not to be interval.[16] The high correlation between alternative scales is illustrated in Figure 4.1, which compares two common types of scaled scores from an algebra test administered to secondary school students by the College Board as part of its Equity 2000 project. The y-axis is a simple number-right score, while the x-axis is proficiency (theta) estimates from a 2-parameter logistic (2-PL) Item Response Theory (IRT) model. Frequency distributions for each scale are shown in the form of kernel plots (smoothed histograms) on the right and top borders of the plot. The relationship between the two scales is clearly nonlinear, but the correlation between them is nonetheless .97 in this sample. This high correlation arises despite the nonlinearity of the relationship because most students are in the central region (as shown by the kernel plots), in which the relationship between the two is quite linear.

However, while the typically high correlation between many scales protects the robustness of many cross-sectional inferences, some inferences, including some important to VAM, may not be robust across scales. For example, consider a hypothetical school district in which some classes include large numbers of students from the extremes of the actual score distribution shown in Figure 4.1, while other classrooms include primarily students from the middle of the

---

[16] Hoover also argued that the developmental scales could be shown not to be interval.

Figure 4.1
Algebra Test Scaled with Simple Number Right Scores and Proficiency
Estimates (theta) from a 2-PL IRT Model (kernel density plots on axes)

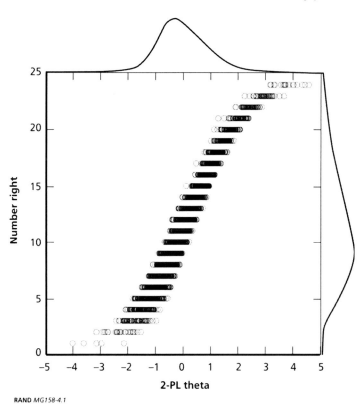

RAND *MG158-4.1*

distribution. Now assume that value added is estimated with both of the two scales. Students at the extremes would show less variance on the number right scale than on the theta scale. If the classes at the extremes showed gains similar to those of the mid-scoring classes on the number-right scale, they would show larger gains than middling classes on the IRT scale. More generally, a lack of robustness in comparisons among teachers will arise if a sufficient number of students score in regions in which the relationships among the scales in question are substantially nonlinear and if students are not randomly distributed among classrooms in terms of prior performance. This may occur when high- and low-scoring groups are compared in a VAM model.

While much of the psychometric literature on the indeterminacy of achievement scales has focused on scaling as such—that is, on the process of placing raw performance onto a reporting scale—some of the indeterminacy of the final scale reflects other aspects of test construction, in particular those pertaining to the mix of dimensions represented in the test. Although most common scaling models treat the construct of interest as unidimensional, this is a simplification. In most cases, a test of any broad domain of achievement, such as mathematics, will assess a variety of different dimensions of performance. The process of constructing the test requires decisions about the relative emphasis given to various aspects of performance. Moreover, the actual emphases inherent in a test may differ independently of the intent of designers because of a variety of factors, including inadvertent overweighting of content (Koretz, McCaffrey, and Hamilton, 2001). The ordering of means, such as district or state means in U.S. comparisons or country means in international comparisons, is sometimes sensitive to these differences in test construction, such as the weighting of content areas within a subject area (e.g., Koretz, 1986; Wolfe, 1997). It is generally assumed that a primary reason for this sensitivity is variations in curricular alignment. That is, even if two tests have largely similar specifications, the specific decisions made to implement them will often make tests differ in their alignment with the curricula of specific jurisdictions.

Treating the resulting scores as representing a single dimension is a useful and defensible simplification for many inferences but may not be for others, including some based on VAM. For example, consider a hypothetical district in which the most able mathematics students in middle school are placed in classes that focus almost entirely on topics newly introduced in middle school, while less proficient students continue focusing substantially on basic arithmetic operations and their application. Now, for the sake of discussion, assume that the test used for VAM purposes focuses substantially on basic skills (as many broad achievement tests in the middle-school grades do). Much of the effectiveness of the teachers of the more able students will escape detection in the VAM analysis because their students are not spending much time studying the elements of performance that have the highest weights on the test. Substituting another test that places more emphasis on higher-level material could substantially change the ranking of teachers.

The severity of this problem will depend not only on the characteristics of tests, but also on the inferences they are used to support. The ideal case for VAM (which is unattainable) would be one in which the test would fully operationalize what all teachers are expected to teach, and test-based inferences about performance would be limited to the domain thus delineated. In this case, differences in alignment would not threaten inferences about the rankings of teachers. Of course, tests generally operationalize the intended domain only incompletely, so one would expect some unwanted variation in rankings as a function of differential alignment between the test and teachers' implemented curricula. The potential threat to estimates of teacher effectiveness, however, goes beyond random differences in alignment and is likely to be systematic. For example, in some instances (such as tracked classes), teachers are expected to teach different things, and the inferences about the performance of one group of students are different from those about other students in the same grade. In such cases, variations in alignment between the single test used in VAM and teachers' curricula may pose a serious threat to the validity of estimates of teacher effectiveness. Thus, the greater the degree of intentional curricular differentiation, the greater the threat to validity. Substantial curricular differentiation is often both intentional and substantial, and it will generally become more severe as students progress through the grades.

Complexities of Vertical Scales. The process of creating a vertical scale, such as those used in nearly all of the VAM models discussed earlier, compounds issues of both dimensionality and scaling. In the case of dimensionality, the issues are similar but more pronounced. In the case of scaling, the construction of a vertical scale creates additional issues.

The process of creating a vertical scale is necessarily ambiguous to the extent that curricula vary across grades. If the domain were truly unidimensional, test items would differ only in terms of their difficulty, their discriminating power, and the lower asymptote of the response function, and they would be substitutable. That is, apart from considerations of reliability and floor and ceiling effects, one could substitute some items designed, say, for fourth grade for others designed for third grade and obtain the same estimates of proficiency,[17] assuming the scaling model fits. However, to the extent that curricula vary across grades, this exchangeability is eroded. This has long been recognized in the field of achievement testing. Thus, users have long been warned that with most test and scaling designs, a student who scores two years above her grade level on the test designed for her grade would not necessarily score at the average on a form designed for two grades higher because of curriculum-related differences in test content (see, for example, Peterson, Kolen, and Hoover, 1989).

As an example of between-grade variations in curricula that could affect inferences about value added, consider middle-school mathematics. In the middle-school grades, students study a wide array of mathematics, commonly ranging from topics in arithmetic introduced in the elementary grades, extensions of those topics (e.g., arithmetic operations with negative numbers), and topics not previously introduced, such as basic algebra. To construct a test battery, one must decide how much weight to give this wide array of topics in the forms administered to each grade. For purposes of illustration, say that one of the choices is how much weight to give several new topic areas, such as algebra, in the eighth-grade form. Suppose that one vendor opts for 20 percent of the items, while another opts for 10 percent of the items. Now suppose that eighth-grade teachers A and B are equally effective but allocate different amounts of their instructional time to the content of these particular items. The two forms will rank the two teachers differently.

The threats to VAM-based inferences from these variations in dimensional mix are likely to vary greatly but may be severe in some

---

[17] That is, the same up to a linear transformation.

instances. It seems apparent that the wider the grade span, the more serious the threat. It also seems likely that the threat becomes larger in the higher grades because of decreasing uniformity of the curriculum. In addition, the severity of the threat is likely to vary with location as a function of curriculum and the heterogeneity of the student population. However, despite the research on the robustness of vertical scales and the smaller literature on the robustness of cohort-to-cohort gains across tests cited below, we are not aware of any studies that specifically examine the robustness of growth estimates or estimated teacher effects to choices in test construction. This should be a priority in further research on VAM.

The general indeterminacy of scale becomes a more complex issue when vertical scales are employed, as in the VAM models discussed above. First, scales that are highly correlated in cross-section may not be as highly correlated across grades. Second, inferences about growth can be sensitive even to linear transformations of scale. For the purposes of VAM, an important indeterminacy that may be merely linear is that vertical scales often show fundamentally different trends in variances across grade levels. A particularly extreme and frequently discussed example was provided by Yen (1986). Figure 4.2 uses numbers taken from Yen (1986), and shows the standard deviations in scaled score points (on the publisher's developmental standard scales) on the mathematics computation subtests of two widely used achievement tests published by the same publisher. The California Achievement Test—Form C (CAT/C), which was scaled using a traditional method known as Thurstone absolute scaling, shows a gradual and monotonic increase in variance across the grades. That is, the distribution of scores "fans out" with age, as faster learners pull progressively farther away from their more slowly learning peers. In contrast, the Comprehensive Test of Basic Skills—Form U (CTBS/U), which was scaled with a more modern 3-parameter logistic IRT model, shows a dramatic narrowing of the distribution throughout the elementary grades.

Figure 4.2
Standard Deviations in Scaled Score Units, CAT/C (Thurstone scaled) and CTBS/U (3-PL IRT scaled), Mathematics Computation

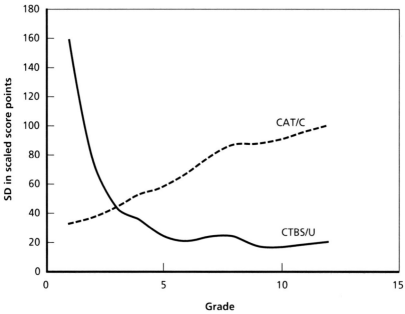

SOURCE: Yen (1986).
RAND MG158-4.2

Clearly, these two scales do not suggest the same inferences about performance. This striking difference in variance trends sparked a sharp debate in the psychometrics field (see, e.g., Burket, 1984; Hoover, 1984a, 1984b; Yen, 1986) over what scale more accurately represented the domain about which inferences are intended and what type of variance trends was most plausible for the inferences that achievement tests are designed to support (Hoover, 1988, and Yen, 1988).

For our purposes, however, the most important issue is simply that the variance trends differ across scales. Clearly, some inferences based on VAM—specifically, those that compare estimated effectiveness of teachers of high- and low-scoring students—will be sensitive to the choice of scale when scales show different variance trends or are not linearly related.

There is at present no consensus in the measurement field that would allow a resolution of this ambiguity. A number of other studies have shown disparities in variance ratios, although the divergence is often much less striking than in Yen's example. However, research does not clearly explain the disparity. The initial debate about the declining variances in the CTBS scale focused on scaling per se—specifically, on the use of 3-parameter logistic (3-PL) IRT models. It has since become less clear, however, what role scaling itself, as opposed to other aspects of vertical linking and test content, plays in determining the pattern of variance changes across grades. For example, Becker and Forsyth (1992) applied both Thurstone and IRT methods to data from a single form, the Iowa Tests of Educational Development administered to students in grades 9–12. This design eliminated two factors that could have contributed to the differences noted in earlier studies: The two types of scaling were performed on data from the same students, and the test was the same across grades and therefore entailed no vertical linking of different forms. Becker and Forsyth (1992) found expanding variances using both scaling methods. Yen and Burket (1997) used simulated data to compare IRT and Thurstone scaling and also found expanding variances with both methods. Williams, Pommerich, and Thissen (1998) scaled the North Carolina End-of-Grade Mathematics Tests using both Thurstone and IRT methods. They found no consistent pattern in the variances yielded by the IRT methods, while the variances obtained with three Thurstone scaling methods generally decreased. The current form of the Terra Nova, the successor form to the CTBS, which is also scaled with a 3-PL model, does not generally show shrinking variances across the grades and indeed shows increasing variances in some instances (CTB/McGraw-Hill, 2001, e.g., Figure 37). There is no commonly accepted understanding of how content, scaling, and linking interact to create these varying patterns.

The primary implication of these findings for our purposes is that some conclusions of VAM studies may be sensitive to choice of scale. A simple simulation confirmed the logical deduction that conclusions about the size of the teacher effect (relative to the total variance of student performance) are not sensitive to variance trends, but inferences that entail comparisons across levels of performance may be quite sensitive. The lack of a clear expectation for variance trends—indeed, the lack of a clear understanding of the factors that contribute to differences in these trends—makes it infeasible at present to reduce this uncertainty. However, it is worth noting that some of the models employed assume an increase in variance across grades.

Inflation of Test Scores

Score inflation refers to increases in scores that do not reflect a commensurate increase in mastery of the domain. It can be caused by a wide variety of teacher behaviors, including simple cheating, inappropriately narrow focus on the content of the test at the expense of other material important for the inference about achievement, teaching test-taking tricks (e.g., process of elimination), and inappropriate focus on substantively unimportant aspects of a particular test.

There have been few large-scale studies of score inflation, but the information currently available suggests that it could pose a serious threat to VAM when scores on high-stakes tests are used as outcomes. Several studies have shown that scores can become seriously inflated under high-stakes conditions (e.g., Jacob, 2002; Klein et al., 2000; Koretz and Barron, 1998; Koretz, Linn, Dunbar, and Shepard, 1991). These studies indicate that score inflation can be several times as large as meaningful gains in test scores. Therefore, any appreciable variability in the extent of inflation could substantially bias the inferences based on VAM. Even a random distribution of inflation would upwardly bias the estimated variance of the teacher effect, and the rankings of many individual teachers would be rendered meaningless. To the extent that the distribution of score inflation is systematically related to important characteristics of teachers or their contexts, inferences about the characteristics of teachers are likely to be severely distorted.

Using Achievement Measures as a Proxy for Measures of Teacher Effectiveness

Summary: Teacher effectiveness might be nonlinearly related to student achievement: A teacher's effectiveness might affect growth differentially for students of different levels of achievement. Thus, a teacher's effects across students might not be constant on the scale of achievement. Moreover, the nonlinear relationship between teacher effects and achievement in one year might not match the relationship in subsequent years, so models for prior-year teachers need to be more general than those currently proposed.

For most current uses of VAM, the actor about whom inferences are drawn is the teacher, not the student. That is, in most cases, the question asked is not whether two increments in scores represent equivalent increases in student performance, but rather whether two increments in scores indicate equivalent amounts of teacher effectiveness. Moreover, these increments are often compared across different levels of the scale. Thus, the inferences rest not only on the assumption that the scale of student performance is interval but also that this maps linearly to the latent scale of effectiveness, so that the scale of teacher effectiveness is also interval.

This assumption about mapping is almost certainly substantially wrong in some instances. For example, assume that a VAM model is used to evaluate the effectiveness of teachers in teaching reading. Assume also that the scale of the reading test used is truly interval. This assumption is unwarranted, but it simplifies the example. Now consider the hypothetical example of two sixth-grade classes. One comprises mostly students at or above grade level, and it makes an average amount of gain over the year. The second includes a large number of students who are far below grade level, many reading at the second-grade level, and it makes well under the average amount of gain over the year. Is it reasonable to conclude that the second teacher is less effective?

Many teachers who have taught remedial reading (including one of the present authors) maintain that this is an extremely difficult type of teaching and that improving the performance of a sixth-grader reading at the second-grade level is much harder than improving the performance of a sixth-grader at the sixth-grade level by a like amount. There are several reasons for this. One is that students who have failed to keep pace in reading have done so for a reason, and some of those reasons (e.g., dyslexia, visual disabilities, or attentional deficits) persist over time. A second reason is that students who have failed in reading often develop counterproductive habits that are difficult to break. A third is that many students who have not been able to learn to read proficiently develop an intense aversion to reading instruction because it becomes strongly associated with failure, embarrassment, and intense frustration. Therefore, even though the two teachers may have been identically effective if they had taught students with similar distributions of initial proficiency, they may obtain much different gains from these two classes.

This illustrates the more general point that the relationship between teacher effectiveness and student score gains may be nonlinear. These nonlinearities may take numerous forms. There may be simple nonlinearities—that is, a unit of effectiveness may produce amounts of gain at different points on the achievement scale. There may be interactions between effectiveness and various attributes of students. That is, some types of students may be harder to teach in the aggregate. There may also be variations that are idiosyncratic to specific teachers. Some teachers, for example, may be most effective with a docile class, while others thrive with a class that is prone to interrupting with challenging questions. Some may be more effective when districts require them to use didactic curricula, whereas others may be more effective with more student-centered, constructivist curricula.

In the presence of this nonlinearity, the score scale would not provide an interval scale of effectiveness even if it were to provide an interval scale of student achievement. That is, the result of such nonlinearities is that teacher effects will not be constant on the scale of student achievement even if they are constant on the scale of teacher effectiveness. This also has implications for the persistence of teacher effects. The relationship between achievement and effectiveness might differ across grades because the distribution of achievement is centered at a different point on the scale at each grade. If the relationship between teacher effects and the current year scores were (nearly) linear, the relationship between teacher effects and subsequent test scores would need to be nonlinear. However, the current models allow at most linear shifts between a teacher's effect in the current and subsequent years.

Although the assumption of a simple, uniform linear relationship between teacher effectiveness and student score gains appears untenable, the degree to which it is a serviceable approximation remains an empirical question. That question should be a focus of future research on VAM models of achievement.

Modeling in the Presence of Measurement Error

Summary: Achievement tests are error-prone measures of achievement. Measurement errors in scaled scores are heteroskedastic—that is, they have greatest variance for students at the high and low extremes of the distribution of true achievement. Models that incorrectly treat the data as homoskedastic can yield unbiased but inefficient estimates of fixed effects. Whether or not these models provide unbiased estimates of random teacher effects is unclear; however, because measurement errors account for a sizable fraction of the variability in scores any systemic errors that result from measurement error are likely to have large effects on inferences about teachers.

As discussed above, test scores are widely accepted as reasonably valid but imprecise measures of true achievement. Many sources contribute to the variability of scores. In this section, we distinguish measurement error from other sources of variance using the following definition: We assume that a test is designed to measure a well-defined construct (e.g., math computation) and that every student has an error-free score for this construct on the scale of measure of the test. For ease of presentation, we call this score the *true level of achievement*. The score can change over time. We consider fluctuations on the scale of a few days or a few weeks transient rather than systematic and thus include them in our definition of measurement error. In addition, we include in our definition variations that result from the construction of a particular test instrument designed to measure the construct of interest (e.g. the number and particular sample of items chosen from a hypothetical domain of all items measuring the construct). It may also be appropriate for some purposes to include in measurement error variations among highly similar tests that measure slightly different constructs. However, in this section, we focus on a single construct and thus do not consider this sort of variation to be a source of measurement error.

The primary challenge posed by measurement error as opposed to other possible sources of error is that the variability of the errors around the true level of achievement is known to depend on that level of achievement. For scaled scores, the measurement error is greatest for extreme values and smallest for values near the mean of the distribution. That is because the expected performance on the test changes slowly as a function of the true achievement level for extreme achievement levels. Thus, it is more difficult to reliably estimate extreme values of true achievement based on the test scores. Alternatively, the expected performance on the test changes more rapidly for students with true achievement near the middle of the distribution, allowing for more-precise distinctions in true level of achievement based on the test scores. Thus, test scores are heteroskedastic with the variance depending on the true level of achievement.

Given that test publishers estimate the standard error of measurement, statistical models could be extended to account for measurement errors and the resulting heteroskedasticity of scores. Such models will be complex because the variability depends on the unobserved true level of achievement. Models that allow the residual variance to be a function of the observed score could serve as a computationally simpler approximation that might provide at least partial benefits.

To date, no VAM applications have explicitly accounted for measurement error or, in particular, the resulting heteroskedasticity in test scores. Multivariate models that ignore heteroskedastic measurement error will yield inefficient but unbiased estimates of fixed parameters. However, it is less clear how accounting for heteroskedasticity might change teacher-effect estimates from multivariate models.

Provided measurement error is mean zero, we expect that, for random-effects models, shrinkage will be greater for teachers with class means in the extremes of the distribution under models that account for heteroskedasticity than under those that do not. For a class with a high average score, students above the classroom mean score will be down-weighted relative to other students in the class and vice versa for a class with a low average score. But it is unclear whether or not models that ignore measurement error and heteroskedasticity will produce estimated teacher effects that differ systematically from the true effects with errors that depend on the true effects. Because measurement errors account for a sizable fraction of the variability in scores, as much as 15 percent for many of the widely used standardized tests, any systemic errors that result from measurement error are likely to have large effects on inferences about teachers.

As discussed above, covariate models that ignore measurement error yield biased estimates of fixed parameters. If students were randomly assigned to classes, measurement would have little systematic effect on estimated teacher effects even though it results in biased estimated of the fixed parameters in the model. However, if student characteristics cluster by class, measurement error will result in bias in which the errors in the teacher effects are positively correlated with student characteristics. Accounting for measurement error in the models could reduce the bias and errors.

Uncertainty About Estimated Effects

In the previous sections, we discussed possible sources of errors in inferences about the variability of teacher effectiveness and about the effectiveness of individual teachers. Much of our discussion focused on issues that would create systematic errors that result from limitations in the statistical models or measures of student performance. We gave little attention to sampling errors that result from the variability from the samples of students and scores used to estimate effects. In this final section of the chapter we discuss uncertainty including sampling error. For VAM models, we believe it is important to consider multiple sources of uncertainty rather than to focus on only sampling error.

Sampling Error

Summary: Sampling error is one of several sources of error in estimated variance components and teacher effects. Sampling errors must be very small for meaningful inferences about some quantities of interest such as teacher rankings. Sampling errors in estimated effects are unlikely to be sufficiently small to support ranking but may be small enough to allow for identifying some teacher effects as distinct from the mean.

Residual variance in student test scores due to measurement error and sources of variability in performance other than teachers, schools, and other factors in the model result in sampling error in estimated model parameters (including variance components) and estimated individual teacher effects. Model parameters depend on variability from the entire sample of students. The sampling error in the estimate of an individual teacher's effect depends on the sampling error of model parameters and the residual variability of the scores for the students in the teacher's class.

The variability in an individual teacher effect due to sampling error will decrease with class size. Estimated effects for teachers with the largest classes will have the smallest variability while estimates for teachers with smaller classes will tend to be more variable. The quality of inferences about teachers will depend on the ratio of the variability due to sampling errors to the variability of the true teacher effects. Given that teacher variability is likely to account for only a modest portion of the total variability in student scores (or gains), residual variability is likely to be much larger than the variability due to teachers. In addition, many teachers teach only moderately small numbers of students. Thus, the variability in sampling error in estimated effects is likely to be large relative to the true variance of teacher effects. For instance, in the example discussed below, variability due to sampling error was between 20 to 40 percent of the estimated variability in teacher effects.

Lockwood, Louis, and McCaffrey (2002) found that, unless the ratio of variance of sampling error in the classroom mean to the variance of teacher effects is less than about 0.1, estimated rankings will be sufficiently imprecise to preclude distinguishing among all but the most extreme teachers. This is a difficult target to achieve. For example, if teachers account for 13 percent of the variability in scores, then classes would need more than 60 students to provide moderately precise rankings (e.g., rankings that are sufficiently precise that the confidence interval for a rank of r would roughly equal about $r \pm n/5$, where n is the number of teachers in the sample). With only 20 students in a class, teachers would need to account for 31 percent of the total variance to provide rankings with this precision.

Although sampling errors might be too great to support inferences about rankings, other useful inferences might be possible. For example, in McCaffrey et al. (2003), we report on a small study which estimated teacher effects for the fourth and fifth grade teachers of 678 students from five schools chosen from a large suburban district. We modeled third, fourth, and fifth grade math scores using the layered model and the persistence model of teacher effects (Eq. 4.5). We used maximum likelihood estimators of the model parameters and EBLUPS to estimate teacher effects. We included in the analysis all records for students with one or more scores, even the 50 percent of records with incomplete data.[18] We assumed missing data were MAR.

We used Bayesian methods to make inferences about the estimated teacher effects so that error estimates account for uncertainty in model parameters. We found that the sampling errors in the estimated teacher effect equaled about 20 to 40 percent of the variance of teacher effects, depending on grade and model. Thus, the sampling error in the estimates would need to be about two to four times smaller to support inference on ranking. However, we found that with both models we identified between one-third and one-fourth of

---

[18] Over 70 percent of tested students have two or more scores. However 113 (15 percent) of the 739 students attending these schools have no tests at all and the study's results apply only to students likely to be tested.

teachers as distinct from the mean—that is, the probability that the teachers' effect was greater than zero was either very high (greater than 0.9), indicating that the teacher was likely to be less effective than average, or very low (less than 0.1), indicating that the teacher was likely to be more effective than average. The two models identified almost all the same teachers as distinct from the mean.

Although this example is limited, it provides an empirical description of the impact of sampling errors on estimated effects—no other studies provide such information. This example is limited by the small size and the purposive nature of the sample. Schools were chosen to have nearly equal proportions of students eligible for free or reduced price lunches. Also, the models do not include any covariates. As discussed, the omitted variables could distort estimated effects, although that is somewhat unlikely to be problematic with this sample given the similarity of student populations across schools. Regardless of these limitations, the example demonstrates that sampling errors can be sufficiently small to support some inferences even if they are too large to support others such as ranking.

While accounting for variability due to sampling error is essential for evaluating errors in estimated teacher effects, estimating variability can be challenging. For fixed- effects models, estimates of the variability due to sampling error (i.e., standard errors) for individual teacher effects are generally produced by statistical software. Conditional on the model, the estimates are probably reasonably accurate estimates of the sampling error. In general, the standard error for a teacher's effect goes down as more student scores are linked to that teacher. For random-effects models, accurate standard errors (assuming the variance components are known) are readily obtained by a standard formula (Searle, Casella, and McCulloch, 1992); more realistic standard errors, which account for the additional uncertainty necessitated by estimating the variance components, require greater consideration. Many authors now suggest using a Bayesian framework for inferences concerning random effects because it accounts for the sampling errors in the parameter estimates and the teacher's sample of students.

Other Sources of Uncertainty

Summary: Sampling errors are only one source of uncertainty in estimated effects. As discussed in much of this chapter, estimated effects are sensitive to model assumptions. Moreover, we have little information for choosing among the alternative models that might impact estimates. Inferences on teacher effects should account for this uncertainty, which is likely to be large until additional research provides more information for supporting modeling decisions.

Much of this chapter has focused on sensitivity of estimated teacher effects and variance components to sources other than sampling errors. Estimates of variability due to sampling error typically are conditioned on the model and the measure and ignore sensitivity to these factors. Given the current uncertainty about the performance of VAM with respect to the persistence of teacher effects, omitted covariates, missing data, and the scale of measure, ignoring uncertainty or error from sources other than sampling error could greatly overstate our confidence in estimated variance components and estimated teacher effects.

At least two approaches to accounting for uncertainty exist. The first is to relax model assumptions by building more-complex models. The persistence model of McCaffrey et al. (2003) is an example of this approach. The model relaxes the assumption of the layered and cross-classified models that teacher effects persist undiminished into the future. Similarly, models theoretically could be expanded to relax such assumptions as modeling the probability that a student completes a test or allowing for heteroskedastic error terms. This approach has limits either because estimating the parameters might be infeasible given the available data and computational tools or because the estimates might be extremely imprecise.

A second approach is to conduct sensitivity analyses to quantify the likely changes to estimates that result from changing model assumptions. Sensitivity analyses are particularly appealing when relaxing model assumptions results in a highly complex model. Also, given the available data, unique estimation of some parameters might be infeasible without strong assumptions. (In statistical jargon, the model requires assumptions to identify some parameters.) For example, most databases contain no information for uniquely estimating the correlation between true teacher effects and aggregate student characteristics, and analysts must make assumptions about this value when estimating teacher effects. Sensitivity analysis might also be preferable when estimates of the parameters of complex models are highly variable as a result of sampling error. In these cases, setting the parameters to reasonable values rather than estimating them might greatly reduce sampling error in estimates of teacher effects. Even though constraining the parameter might introduce or increase bias or systematic errors, this approach might reduce overall error if the increase in bias is offset by a greater reduction in sampling error. Overall error is typically calculated as the expected value of the squared difference between the estimate and the true value, and it equals variance plus squared bias.

Additional research is necessary to develop methods for incorporating the uncertainty of estimates identified via sensitivity analysis into our inferences about teacher effects and variance components. Recent work in the field of epidemiology (Lash, 2003; Greenland, 2003) might be applicable. Bayesian methods look promising because model assumptions can be specified via prior distributions on model parameters, and relaxation of models assumption can be conducted on a continuum by making prior distributions more or less informative (Lindley, 2000). Also in the Bayesian framework (relative) posterior probabilities of models can be calculated, and the resulting model-specific inferences can be combined to make aggregate inferences that reflect model uncertainty (Hoeting et al., 1999). Additional empirical research into the sensitivity of estimates to the factors identified in this chapter will be useful for designing sensitivity analyses and determining plausible values for setting model parameters, or in Bayesian analyses for providing well informed prior distributions for model parameters.

CHAPTER FIVE

Discussion

What Have We Learned?

VAM is currently of great interest to researchers and policymakers both because it is believed to provide a means of separating the effects of schools and teachers from those of such noneducational factors as student background and because it appears to demonstrate the importance of teachers to student achievement. Policymakers and researchers have expressed hope that the use of VAM in teacher evaluation and accountability systems will contribute to improved decision-making and that it will lead to increased knowledge regarding the factors that contribute to effective teaching. Despite this growing enthusiasm, however, the existing research base on VAM suggests that more work is needed before the techniques can be used to support important decisions about teachers or schools. There is currently no single, agreed-upon approach for using VAM to estimate teacher or school effects. Rather, as we have demonstrated, VAM refers to a diverse class of models with many possible paths from data to estimates. As a result, researchers face several important decision points in translating a given research or policy question into a specific model, and they must address several issues that can affect the validity of VAM estimates.

Our review of VAM revealed that accurate and precise estimation of teacher effects is very challenging. Many interrelated factors contribute in complex ways to teacher-effect estimates, and little is currently known about the actual sensitivity of VAM estimates to many of these factors. In this document, we have described a number of these factors and the potential challenges they present to researchers and other potential users of VAM as they decide whether and how to use VAM in their work. The key conclusions of our research regarding these issues may be summarized as follows.

First, users of VAM need to provide explicit definitions of the causal teacher effects that are the target of inference. A causal effect is the comparison of a student's achievement with the current teacher to achievement under a plausible alternative. There is no single plausible alternative for a specific teacher's effect, and users of VAM must carefully state the alternative that is of interest. For example, is it other teachers in the school, school district, or state? Also, a teacher's effect might not be constant across students, so users must identify which students are being considered. Without such explicit definitions, it is impossible to evaluate estimated effect or make meaningful inferences about teachers.

Second, we have identified a number of possible threats to the robustness of conclusions based on current VAM models. These include threats stemming from differences in test construction and scaling, as well as those resulting from certain modeling decisions, such as the decision to assume that teacher effects do not diminish in the layered and cross-classified models. The impact of these decisions is unknown but could be large enough to undermine the utility of some VAM-based inferences, particularly those that contrast teachers of students having very different levels of achievement. A particular concern is missing data, which are pervasive in most student achievement databases. Students are sometimes not tested, and they often transfer in and out of schools. Many state and district data systems are not capable of tracking students who change schools, which can result in a substantial amount of missing data. Because missing data are so common, errors in model assumptions about the nature of missing data could have a large impact on VAM estimates.

Third, in contrast to what the term value-added implies and contradictory to the primary source of enthusiasm for these methods,

VAM models do not resolve completely the issue of bias from omitted variables. This problem is exacerbated by the stratified nature of the U.S. education system—that is, the fact that students are clustered within schools by race/ethnicity, income, and other background factors associated with achievement. We have found in limited settings that individual background characteristics, as well as contextual effects (e.g., the average socioeconomic status within a school or classroom), predict level and gain scores. Because true teacher effects might be correlated with the characteristics of the students they teach, current VAM approaches cannot separate any existing contextual effects from these true teacher effects. Existing research is not sufficient for determining the generalizability of this finding or the severity of the actual problems associated with omitted background variables.

Finally, our analysis and simulations demonstrate that VAM-based rankings of teachers are highly unstable, and that only large differences in estimated impact are likely to be detectable given the effects of sampling error and other sources of uncertainty. Interpretations of differences among teachers based on VAM estimates should be made with extreme caution.

What Do We Know About Teacher Effects?

Given these concerns, what do the current literature and studies of teacher effects tell us about teachers? Even though the current research does not address or overcome all the challenges presented herein, we cautiously conclude from our review of the literature that teachers differentially affect student achievement. Across diverse studies using different age cohorts, different models and statistical approaches, and different types of achievement measures, the studies all find nonzero teacher effects. Furthermore, the extensive simulation studies we conducted imply that some of the findings from the literature would be unlikely to result solely from omitted variables, bias, or confounding, suggesting that these findings are truly the results of teacher effects and not other factors. However, because of various limitations to each study, the literature provides little convincing evidence on the magnitude of the typical teacher effect or relative importance of teachers as a source of variability in student achievement.

Generally, given the current state of knowledge about VAM, we expect that some efforts to estimate teacher effects could provide useful information on teachers, whereas other efforts would most likely provide estimates with large errors and which are highly sensitive to model assumptions and changes in measurement. VAM estimation is likely to provide estimates that are least sensitive to the factors described above when the distribution of students and teachers across classrooms closely approximates the distribution that would result from random assignment of students and teachers. School districts with homogeneous populations of students, curriculums that are consistent across classes in the same grade, and a stable population that does not transfer into or out of the district are likely to be closest to this ideal. School systems serving diverse population that are stratified by schools—such as large urban populations that include both poor inner-city schools and affluent suburban schools—will be most sensitive to omitted covariates, changes in scaling, and changes in topic mix (because curriculum difference will exist). Such school systems also typically serve highly mobile populations that miss testing. On the other hand, very stable and homogeneous school systems might attract teachers of similar effectiveness and thus might provide poor measures of the true variability of teachers.

Recommendations for Future Research

Clearly, much remains unknown about VAM. But a systematic approach to future research on VAM could fill the gaps in our knowledge and might increase the utility of VAM for evaluating teachers. We suggest the following areas for future research.

1. Develop Databases That Can Support VAM Estimation of Teacher Effects

The key to a greater understanding of VAM is more empirical studies. Because studies begin with data, the first step toward future research should be the development of databases to support VAM. The data must be longitudinal with at least annual test scores on students from measures of achievement that have well-understood psychometric properties. The databases must also include details on the links between students, teachers, and schools and include a broad collection of measures of student characteristics.

2. Develop Computational Tools for Fitting VAM

Readily available commercial software can fit the multivariate layered and cross-classified models only to relatively small datasets. No readily available software can fit the persistence model of McCaffrey et al. (2003). Such software is necessary if VAM is to be tested by more jurisdictions. In addition, tools are necessary to extend the models to allow for features such as heteroskedasticity of residual errors within a grade and missing data that are MNAR.

3. Link VAM Teacher-Effect Estimates to Alternative Measures of Teacher Effectiveness

We have noted that there is little research linking teacher-effect estimates to specific characteristics or practices of teachers, and the research that has been conducted has not shed much light on the major sources of variability in teacher effects. The fact that we can estimate effects but cannot specify what attributes those effects are capturing limits the utility of these estimates for policy and practice. In addition, it calls into question both the meaning of outcomes-based definitions of teacher effects and the accuracy of the current estimates. Before VAM can be used to help teachers improve their practices or to contribute to more effective teacher preparation or professional development, users need to understand what factors contribute to teacher effectiveness. Research linking VAM estimates to characteristics of teachers such as years of experience or credentialing status (similar to that described by Rivkin, Hanushek, and Kain, 2000) is a starting point, but existing research suggests that these easily measured characteristics are unlikely to be the major source of variation in teacher effectiveness. Additional work is needed to identify likely attributes, develop valid measures of them, and link them to VAM estimates. Much of this work is likely to be conducted outside the arena of VAM research. For example, Cohen, Raudenbush, and Ball (2003) summarize some of the factors that appear to contribute to effective instruction and discuss the need to develop measures and incorporate them into research that links resources to student achievement. Additional research that addresses these factors in the context of VAM will be critical if VAM is to contribute to improved teacher training or staffing decisions.

4. Empirically Evaluate the Potential Sources of Errors We Have Identified

Empirical evaluations do not exist for many of the potential sources of error we have identified. Studies need to be conducted to determine how these factors contribute to estimated teacher effects and to determine the conditions that exacerbate or mitigate the impact these factors have on teacher effects. Some of the key factors to evaluate include the following.

Impact of Different Methods of Constructing and Scaling Tests. A number of topics related to test construction and scaling might affect VAM estimates and deserve additional study. Although research has addressed the robustness of vertical scales and, to a lesser degree, of cohort-to-cohort gains across tests, there is a need for VAM research to understand the degree to which choices in scaling and test construction influence estimated teacher effects as well as estimates of achievement growth. Studies comparing estimates made under alternative scaling and with alternative measures would be one component to such research. Understanding how the nature of the achievement measures affects inferences from VAM is particularly important in light of the current emphasis on criterion-referenced reporting of scores on state accountability tests, since this form of reporting creates additional challenges that have not been well explored.

In addition, we have discussed ways in which the assumption of a uniform linear relationship between teacher effectiveness and student score gains may not be appropriate in most modeling situations. However, there is little empirical research that sheds light on the degree to which this assumption may provide a reasonable approximation for common VAM applications, or on the conditions necessary to make the assumption tenable. Models that allow teacher effects to vary across students, such as models with interactions between teacher and student attributes, are a possible method to explore this complex issue. Other important areas of future research on testing are the effects of differential test-curriculum match and the effects of timing of test administration.

Inclusion of Student Covariates. As we have shown, the effects of including student covariates in models depend on a number of factors. In some cases, their exclusion is unlikely to affect the estimates; in others, omitted covariates may be problematic. In addition, even when student-level covariates appear to be unimportant, contextual effects represented by averages of these covariates across teachers or schools may be correlated with teacher-effect estimates (see also McCaffrey et al., 2003). There is no straightforward way to control for group-level covariates. Research into the existence, magnitude, and variability of contextual effects on scores and gain scores for different populations needs to be conducted. Research should also identify data sources and methods that can address the problem of contextual effects in the presence of correlations between true teacher effects and student covariates. For example, the sensitivity of estimates to unobserved student covariates could be studied by extending the methods by Rosenbaum (2002, Chapter 4) for estimating causal effects of treatment using unmatched treatment and comparison groups.

Impact of Missing Data. Although we expect missing data are likely to be pervasive, there is little systematic discussion of the extent or nature of missing data in test score databases. Studies that model the probability of missing test scores and allow that probability to depend on the values of the unobserved scores, possibly via methods suggested by Little (1995) or Diggle and Kenward (1994), could prove valuable for determining the impact of missing data and the validity of the assumptions behind all the currently used models.

Contributions of Prior-Year Teachers to Current-Year Scores. A model for estimating the persistence of teacher effects into future-year scores exists and should be used to explore the contributions of prior-year teachers to current-year scores. Estimates from such models will support efforts to determine the bias from assuming that effects remain undiminished, as is done by the layered and cross-classified models. Also, the persistence of effects is of interest for guiding policy on staffing and class assignment.

5. Estimate the Prevalence of Factors That Contribute to the Sensitivity of Teacher-Effect Estimates

The research just described will identify factors demonstrated to affect estimated teacher effects. However, the prevalence of such factors will be largely unknown. A broad survey across diverse school districts to assess the existence of conditions that mitigate or exacerbate the effect of each factor identified in the studies suggested above would be a valuable contribution toward assessing the likely impact of these factors on teacher-effect estimates.

Another method for determining the prevalence of factors contributing to teacher effects is replication of studies estimating teacher effects and conducting sensitivity analyses. To the extent possible, studies should follow guidelines to support post hoc meta-analyses to determine the likely size and variability in sensitivity of estimates to the various factors identified through other research. Meta-regression approaches (Morton et al., 2003) could be used to determine which characteristics of school systems and the populations they serve are associated with variability in the sensitivity of estimated effects.

6. Incorporate Decision Theory into VAM

Policymakers desire VAM estimates to evaluate teachers and make decisions about teachers' performance through formal or informal means. Studies that incorporate VAM into a decision-theoretic framework could lead to decisions with lower costs for all parties involved. Researchers should work with policymakers to elicit the decision of interest in a formal framework. Then they should work with policymakers to determine the costs of making errors in these decisions. For example, the possible costs to the teacher, school, or students from determining that a teacher is highly effective when in reality he is not would be significant. Although complete specification of costs is likely to prove impossible, better understanding of the relative cost of various errors could lead to greatly improved decisions.

From these descriptions of costs, researchers could then develop loss-functions—quantitative descriptions of the loss a decisionmaker incurs for taking a particular action for a given state of events. Estimators of teacher effects that minimize expected loss could be developed. For example, if the policymaker is interested in rewarding highly effective teachers, the loss from incorrect identification of teachers as highly effective could be determined and estimators that provide more-precise estimates for teachers who are truly highly effective could be developed, possibly along the lines of the methods of Stern and Cressie (1999).

7. Use Research and Auxiliary Data to Inform Modeling Choices

The information gathered by the research we outline above could be used to inform modeling choices for making teacher-effect estimates. For example, if studies repeatedly show that teacher effects do in fact persist nearly undiminished, then the layered model might be used rather than the persistence model. In a Bayesian context, the information from prior research could be used to specify prior distributions on model parameters and models to reduce uncertainty in resulting estimates. Similarly, alternative measures of teacher effectiveness—for instance, qualitative evaluation conducted by the principals—could provide prior probability distributions for individual teacher effects.

Recommendations for the Use of VAM in Policy and Practice

The research base is currently insufficient for us to recommend the use of VAM for high-stakes decisions. In particular, the likely biases from the factors we discussed in Chapter Four are unknown, and there are no existing methods to account for either the bias or the uncertainty that the possibility of bias presents for estimates. Furthermore, the variability due to sampling error of individual teacher-effect estimates depends on a number of factors—including class sizes and the number of years of test-score data available for each teacher—and is likely to be relatively large. Similarly, rankings of teachers should be avoided because of lack of stability of estimated rankings.

At the current time, VAM may show promise for lower-stakes, diagnostic purposes. Examples include identifying teachers who might be low or high performing so that follow-ups can be done to verify the VAM findings. Inferences would need to be circumspect because of possible bias or sensitivity to the measure, but they could be a starting point for administrators (such as principals or superintendents) to target teachers for more thorough review.

However, other methods for using test scores to evaluate schools or teachers are currently being incorporated into accountability systems that carry high stakes, most recently as a result of No Child Left Behind. These other methods are affected by many of the problems we have discussed with respect to VAM, as well as by additional problems (such as cohort-to-cohort differences in student characteristics) that are not inherent in VAM. It is not clear whether using VAM in those situations would create any additional risk of harm beyond what is already inherent in most test-based accountability systems—VAM might actually provide less-biased and more-precise assessments of teacher effects. We know very little about how alternate methods compare with one another, and there is a particular need for comparisons of VAM approaches to constructing accountability indices with the more commonly used approach of cohort-to-cohort gains.

If test-based accountability remains an instrument of education policy, we recommend that, as policymakers evaluate alternative models for school or teacher accountability, VAM should be given serious consideration even in light of its limitations. Policymakers should carefully weigh its strengths and weaknesses against those of the alternatives and choose a method that is likely to provide the best information with the least possibility for incorrect inference given the current state of knowledge. Any resulting implementation of VAM or any other method, however, should be accompanied by sensitivity analyses and studies of the effects of the system on students, teachers, and schools. It is particularly critical that the techniques adopted by districts or states be subjected to outside scrutiny. Therefore, users of

VAM should make their data and methods accessible to other users and researchers. And, as discussed above, a major focus of any re-analyses of such data should be a comparison of alternate models in an effort to understand the effects of various assumptions on the modeling results.

Perhaps the most important recommendation for ensuring appropriate use of VAM now and in the future is for policymakers, practitioners, and VAM researchers to work together so that research is informed by the practical needs and constraints facing users of VAM, and so that implementation of the models is informed by an understanding of what kinds of inferences and decisions the research currently supports. Researchers' efforts could benefit immensely from conversations with policymakers and practitioners to clarify how the models will be used. Not only should researchers make their results accessible to nontechnical users, but they should also provide guidance to potential users on such issues as the types of data that districts and states should collect and the ways in which VAM does or does not support particular inferences. Collaboration between those who study VAM and those who use it in practice is critical for advancing the state of knowledge and improving the utility of this approach.

Summary

We have provided a systematic review of the issues that are likely to affect VAM estimates. Analysts creating estimates should conduct sensitivity analyses and provide the necessary information for others to evaluate the uncertainty of estimates arising from the factors we have discussed. Analysts should also provide descriptions of the populations and details on the targets of inference and modeling choices so that the impact of these factors can be fully evaluated. In the end, however, it is the job of policymakers and educators to define their inferential goals and to decide what kinds of uncertainty are acceptable and what kinds are not. Analysts can then develop the best models to meet those requirements.

Bibliography

Alexander, K.L., Entwisle, D.R., & Olson, L.S. (2001). Schools, achievement, and inequality: A seasonal perspective. *Educational Evaluation and Policy Analysis*, 23(2), 171–191.

Allison, P.D. (1990). Change scores as dependent variables in regression analysis. *Sociological Methodology*, 20, 93–114.

Angrist, J.D., Imbens, G.W., & Rubin, D.B. (1996). Identification of causal effects using instrumental variables. *Journal of the American Statistical Association*, 91, 444–455.

Ballou, D., Sanders, W., & Wright, P. (2003). Controlling for students' background in value-added assessment of teachers. *Journal of Educational and Behavioral Statistics,* forthcoming.

Becker, D.F. & Forsyth, R.A. (1992). An empirical investigation of Thurstone and IRT methods of scaling achievement tests. *Journal of Educational Measurement,* 29(4), 341–354.

Bock, R., Wolfe, R., & Fisher, T. (1996). *A Review and Analysis of the Tennessee Value-Added Assessment System.* Technical Report, Tennessee Office of Education Accountability, Nashville, TN.

Borman, G.D., Stringfield, S.C., & Slavin, R.E. (Eds.). (2002). *Title I: Compensatory Education at the Crossroads: Sociocultural, Political, and Historical Studies in Education.* Mahwah, NJ: Lawrence Erlbaum Associates, Inc.

Bryk, A.S. & Weisberg, H.I. (1976). Value-added analysis: A dynamic approach to the estimation of treatment effects. *Journal of Educational Statistics*, 1, 127–155.

Bryk, A.S. & Weisberg, H.I. (1977). Use of nonequivalent control group design when subjects are growing. *Psychological Bulletin*, 84, 950–962.

Burket, G.R. (1984). Response to Hoover. *Educational Measurement: Issues and Practice,* 3(4), 15–16.

Carlin, B.P. & Louis, T.A. (2000). *Bayes and Empirical Bayes Methods for Data Analysis.* (2nd ed.). New York: Chapman & Hall.

Cohen, D.K., Raudenbush, S.W., & Ball, D.L. (2003). Resources, instruction, and research. *Educational Evaluation and Policy Analysis,* 25, 119–142.

Coleman, J.S., Campbell, E.Q., Hobson, C.J., McPartland, J., Mood, A.M., Weinfeld, F.D., & York, R.L. (1966). *Equality of Educational Opportunity.* Washington, D.C.: U.S. Government Printing Office.

CTB/McGraw-Hill (2001). *Terra Nova: Technical Report.* Monterey, CA: author.

DebRoy, S. & Bates, D. (2003) Computational methods for multiple level linear mixed-effects models. University of Wisconsin-Madison, Department of Statistics Technical Report No. 1076. http://www.stat.wisc.edu/~bates/reports/TR1076_letter.pdf.

Diggle, P. & Kenward, M.G. (1994). Informative drop-out in longitudinal data analysis. *Applied Statistics,* 43, 49–73.

Feldt, L.S. (1958). A comparison of the precision of three experimental designs employing a concomitant variable. *Psychometrika,* 23, 335–353.

General Assembly of Pennsylvania (2002). *House Bill No. 45,* October 9.

Goldhaber, D.D. & Brewer, D.J. (2000). Does teacher certification matter? High school teacher certification status and student achievement. *Educational Evaluation and Policy Analysis,* 22, 129–145.

Greene, W.H. (1997). *Econometric Analysis.* (3rd ed.). Upper Saddle River, NJ: Prentice Hall.

Greenland, S. (2003). The need for multiple-bias modeling in observational studies. Joint Statistical Meetings, August 3, 2003, San Francisco California.

Greenwald, R., Hedges, L.V., & Laine, R.D. (1996). The effect of school resources on student achievement. *Review of Educational Research,* 66, 361–396.

Hanushek, E. (1972). *Education and Race.* Lexington, MA: D.C. Heath and Company.

Hanushek, E. (1979). Conceptual and empirical issues in the estimation of educational production functions. *Journal of Human Resources,* 14(1), 351–388.

Hanushek, E.A. (1981). Throwing money at schools. *Journal of Policy Analysis and Management, 1,* 19–41.

Hanushek, E.A. (1991). When school finance "reform" may not be good policy. *Harvard Journal on Legislation, 28,* 423–456.

Hanushek, E.A. (1996). A more complete picture of school resource policies. *Review of Educational Research, 66,* 397–409.

Hedeker, D. & Gibbons, R.D. (1997). Application of random-effects pattern-mixture models for missing data in longitudinal studies. *Psychological Methods, 2,* 64–78.

Hoeting, J., Madigan, D., Raftery, A., & Volinsky, C. (1999). Bayesian model averaging. *Statistical Science, 14,* 382–401.

Holland, P.W. (1986). Statistics and causal inference. *Journal of the American Statistical Association, 81,* 945–960.

Hoover, H.D. (1984a). The most appropriate scores for measuring educational development in the elementary schools: GEs. *Educational Measurement: Issues and Practice, 3*(4), 8–14.

Hoover, H.D. (1984b). Rejoinder to Burket. *Educational Measurement: Issues and Practice, 3*(4), 16–18.

Hoover, H.D. (1988). Growth expectations for low-achieving students: A reply to Yen. *Educational Measurement: Issues and Practice, 7*(4), 21–23.

Jacob, B. (2002). "Accountability, Incentives and Behavior: Evidence from School Reform in Chicago." Cambridge, MA: National Bureau of Economic Research, NBER Working Paper #8968.

Kain, J.F. (1998). *The Impact of Individual Teachers and Peers on Individual Student Achievement,* paper presented at the Association for Public Policy Analysis and Management 20th Annual Research Conference, New York, October 31.

Kane, T.J. & Staiger, D.O. (2001, March). *Improving School Accountability Measures.* Cambridge, MA: National Bureau of Economic Research.

Klein, S.P., Hamilton, L.S., McCaffrey, D.F., & Stecher, B.M. (2000). *What Do Test Scores in Texas Tell Us?* Santa Monica, CA: RAND Corporation, IP-202.

Koretz, D. (1986). *Trends in Educational Achievement.* Washington, DC: U.S. Congressional Budget Office.

Koretz, D. & Barron, S.I. (1998). *The Validity of Gains on the Kentucky Instructional Results Information System (KIRIS).* Santa Monica, CA: RAND Corporation, MR-1014-EDU.

Koretz, D., Linn, R.L., Dunbar, S.B., & Shepard, L.A. (1991). The effects of high-stakes testing: Preliminary evidence about generalization across tests. In R.L. Linn (chair), *The Effects of High Stakes Testing*, symposium presented at the annual meetings of the American Educational Research Association and the National Council on Measurement in Education, Chicago, April.

Koretz, D., McCaffrey, D., & Hamilton, L. (2001). *Toward a Framework for Validating Gains Under High-Stakes Conditions.* Los Angeles: Center for the Study of Evaluation, University of California. CSE Technical Report 551.

Kupermintz, H. (2002) *Teacher Effects As a Measure of Teacher Effectiveness: Construct Validity Considerations in TVAAS (Tennessee Value-Added Assessment System).* Los Angeles: Center for the Study of Evaluation, University of California. CSE Technical Report 563.

Lash, T. (2003). Monte-Carlo sensitivity analysis of sytematic errors in observational epidemiologic data. Joint Statistical Meetings, August 3, 2003, San Francisco, California.

Ligon, G. & Paredes, V. (1992). Student mobility rate: A moving target. Paper presented at the annual meeting of the American Educational Research Association, San Francisco, April.

Lindley, D.V. (2000). The philosophy of statistics. *The Statistician*, 49, 293–337.

Linn, R.L. (2000). Assessments and accountability. *Educational Researcher*, 29(2), 4–14.

Linn, R.L., Dunbar, S.B., Harnisch, D.L., & Hastings, C.N. (1982). The validity of the Title I evaluation and reporting system. In E.R. House, S. Mathison, J. Pearsol, & H. Preskill (Eds.), *Evaluation Studies Review Annual*, Vol. 7, Beverly Hills, CA: Sage Publications, 427–442.

Little, R.J.A. (1993). Pattern-mixture models for multivariate incomplete data. *Journal of the American Statistical Association*, 88, 125–134.

Little, R.J.A. (1995). Modeling the drop-out mechanism in repeated-measures studies. *Journal of the American Statistical Association*, 90, 1112–1121.

Little, R.J.A. & Rubin, D.B. (2002). *Statistical Analysis with Missing Data.* (2nd ed.) New York, Chichester: John Wiley & Sons.

Lockwood, J., Louis, T., & McCaffrey, D. (2002). Uncertainty in rank estimation: Implications for value-added modeling accountability systems. *Journal of Educational and Behavioral Statistics*, 27(3), 255–270.

Lord, F.M. (1969). Statistical adjustments when comparing preexisting groups. *Psychological Bulletin*, 72(5), 336–337.

McCaffrey, D.F., Lockwood, J., Koretz, D., Louis, T.A., & Hamilton, L. (2003). Models for value-added modeling of teacher effects. *Journal of Educational and Behavioral Statistics*, forthcoming.

McLanahan, S. (1997). Parent absence or poverty. In Greg Duncan and Jeanne Brooks-Gunn (Eds.), *Consequences of Growing Up Poor, New York;* Russell Sage, 35–48.

Mendro, R., Jordan, H., Gomez, E., Anderson, M., & Bembry, K. (1998). An application of multiple linear regression in determining longitudinal teacher effectiveness. Paper presented at the 1998 Annual Meeting of the AERA, San Diego, CA.

Meyer, R. (1997). Value-added indicators of school performance: A primer. *Economics of Education Review*, 16, 183–301.

Miller, J.W., McKenna, B.A., & McKenna, M.C. (1998). A comparison of alternatively and traditionally prepared teachers. *Journal of Teacher Education,* 49, 165–176.

Monk, D.H. (1994). Subject area preparation of secondary mathematics and science teachers and student achievement. *Economics of Education Review*, 13, 125–145.

Morton, S.C., Adams, J.L., Suttorp, M., & Shekelle, P. (2003). *Meta-Regression Approaches: What, Why, When And How?* Rockville, MD: Agency for Healthcare Research and Quality, U.S. Dept. of Health and Human Services.

Murnane, R.J. (1975). *The Impact of School Resources on the Learning of Inner City Children.* Cambridge, MA: Ballinger Publishing Co.

Pedersen, E., Faucher, T.A., & Eaton, W.W. (1978). A new perspective on the effects of first-grade teachers on children's subsequent adult status. *Harvard Educational Review,* 48(1), 1–31.

Peterson, N.S., Kolen, M.J., & Hoover, H.D. (1989). Scaling, norming, and equating. In R.L. Linn (Ed.), *Educational Measurement: Third Edition.* New York: American Council on Education and Macmillan Publishing Company, pp. 201–222.

Prospects: The Congressionally Mandated Study of Educational Opportunity. U.S. Department of Education, Office of Educational Research and Improvement. Online at http://www.ed.gov/index.jsp.

Rasbash, J. & Goldstein, H. (1994). Efficient analysis of mixed hierarchical and cross-classified random structures using a multilevel model. *Journal of Educational and Behavioral Statistics*, 19, 337–350.

Raudenbush, S. & Bryk, A. (2002). *Hierarchical Linear Models: Applications and Data Analysis Methods* (2nd ed.). Newbury Park, CA: Sage Publications.

Rivers, J.C. (1999). *The Impact of Teacher Effect on Student Math Competency Achievement*, dissertation, University of Tennessee, Knoxville. Ann Arbor, MI: University Microfilms International, 9959317, 2000.

Rivkin, S.G., Hanushek, E.A., & Kain, J.F. (2000). "Teachers, Schools, and Academic Achievement." Cambridge, MA: National Bureau of Economic Research, NBER Working Paper # W6691.

Roberts, G.O. & Stramer, O. (2001). On inference for partially observed nonlinear diffusion models using the Metropolis-Hastings algorithm. *Biometrika*, 88, 603–621.

Robins, J.M., Rotnitzky, A., & Zhao, L.P. (1995). Analysis of semiparametric regression models for repeated outcomes in the presence of missing data. *Journal of the American Statistical Association*, 90, 106–121.

Robinson, G.K. (1991). That BLUP is a good thing: The estimation of random effects. *Statistical Science*, 6, 15–32.

Rogosa, D.R. (1995). Myths and methods: "Myths about longitudinal research" plus supplemental questions. In J.M. Gottman (Ed.), *The Analysis of Change*. Mahwah, NJ: Lawrence Erlbaum Associates, 3–66.

Rogosa, D.R., Brandt, D., & Zimowski, M. (1982). A growth curve approach to measurement of change. *Psychological Bulletin*, 92, 72–748.

Rogosa, D.R. & Willett, J.B. (1982). Understanding correlates of change by modeling individual differences in growth. *Psychometrika*, 50, 203–228.

Rosenbaum, P.R. (2002). *Observational Studies*. (2nd ed.) New York: Springer-Verlag Inc.

Rosenbaum, P.R. & Rubin, D.B. (1983). The central role of the propensity score in observational studies for causal effects. *Biometrika*, 70, 41–55.

Rowan, B., Correnti, R., & Miller, R.J. (2002). What large-scale survey research tells us about teacher effects on student achievement: Insights from the *Prospects* study of elementary schools. *Teachers College Record*, 104, 1525–1567.

Rubin, D.B. (1974). Estimating causal effects of treatment in randomized and nonrandomized studies. *Journal of Education Psychology*, 66, 688–701.

Rubin, D.B., Stern, H.S., & Vehovar, V. (1995). Handling "Don't know" survey responses: The case of the Slovenian plebiscite. *Journal of the American Statistical Association*, 90, 822–828.

Sanders, W. & Horn, S. (1998). Research findings from the Tennessee value-added assessment system (TVAAS) database: Implications for educational evaluation and research. *Journal of Personnel Evaluation in Education*, 12(3), 247–256.

Sanders, W.L. & Rivers, J.C. (1996). *Cumulative and residual effects of teachers on future student academic achievement.* Knoxville, TN: University of Tennessee Value-Added Research Center.

Sanders, W., Saxton, A., & Horn, B. (1997). The Tennessee Value-Added Assessment System: A quantitative outcomes-based approach to educational assessment. In J. Millman (Ed.), *Grading Teachers, Grading Schools: Is Student Achievement a Valid Evaluational Measure?* Thousand Oaks, CA: Corwin Press, Inc., 137–162.

Schafer, J.L. (1998). *Some Improved Procedures for Linear Mixed Models.* The Pennsylvania State University, Department of Statistics.

Searle, S., Casella, G., & McCulloch, C. (1992). *Variance Components.* New York: John Wiley & Sons.

Shkolnik, J., Hikawa, H., Suttorp, M., Lockwood, J.R., Stecher, B., & Bohrnstedt, G. (2002). Appendix D: The Relationship between teacher characteristics and student achievement in reduced-size classes: A study of 6 California districts. In G. Bohrnstedt & B. Stecher (Eds.), *What We Have Learned About Class Size Reduction in California: Technical Appendix.* Sacramento, CA: California Department of Education, D1–D22.

Smith, B. (1998). *It's About Time: Opportunities to Learn in Chicago's Elementary Schools.* Chicago, IL: Consortium on Chicago School Research. http://www.consortium-chicago.org/publications/pdfs/p0f03.pdf.

Spencer, B.D. (1983). On interpreting test scores as social indicators: Statistical considerations. *Journal of Educational Measurement*, 20(4), 317–333.

Stern, H. & Cressie N. (1999). Inference for extremes in disease mapping. In A. Lawson, A. Biggeri, D. Bohning, E. Lesaffre, J.-F. Viel, & R. Bertollini (Eds.), *Disease Mapping and Risk Assessment for Public Health.* Chichester: John Wiley & Sons, pp. 63–84.

Stevens, S.S. (1946). On the theory of scales of measurement. *Science,* 103(2684), 677–680.

Stevens, S.S. (1968). Measurement, statistics, and the schemapiric view. *Science,* 161 (3844), 849–856.

Thum, Y.M. (2003). *Measuring Progress Towards a Goal: Estimating Teacher Productivity using a Multivariate Multilevel Model for Value-Added Analysis.* A Milken Family Foundation Report. http:www.gleis. ucla.edu/faculty/thum/Papers/SMR-REV.pdf.

U.S. Department of Education, National Center for Education Statistics. (2002). 1998 reading assessments. Washington, D.C.: U.S. Government Printing Office. http://nces.ed.gov/nationsreportcard/naepdata/getdata. asp.

Wang, M.C., Haertel, G.D., & Walberg, H.J. (1993). Toward a knowledge base for school learning. *Review of Educational Research,* 63(3), 249–294.

Webster, W. & Mendro, R. (1997). The Dallas value-added accountability system. In J. Millman (Ed.), *Grading Teachers, Grading Schools: Is Student Achievement a Valid Evaluation Measure?* Thousand Oaks, CA: Corwin Press, Inc., pp. 81–99.

Webster, W., Mendro, R., Orsak, T., & Weerasinghe, D. (1998). An Application of Hierarchical Linear Modeling to the Estimation of School and Teacher Effects. Paper presented at the annual meeting of the American Educational Research Association, April 13–17, 1998, San Diego, CA.

West, S.G., Biesanz, J.C., & Pitts, S.C. (2000). Causal inference and generalization in field settings experimental and quasi-experimental designs. In H.T. Reis & C.M. Judd (Eds.), *Handbook of Research Methods in Social and Personality Psychology.* New York: Cambridge University Press, pp. 40–88.

Williams, V.S.L., Pommerich, M., and Thissen, D. (1998). A comparison of developmental scales based on Thurstone methods and Item Response Theory. *Journal of Educational Measurement,* 35(2), 93–107.

Wolfe, R. (1997). Country-by-item interactions: Problems with content validity in scaling. In *Validity in Cross-National Assessments: Problems and Pitfalls.* Symposium presented at the annual meeting of the American Educational Research Association, Chicago, April 27.

Wright, S.P., Horn, S.P., & Sanders, W.L. (1997). Teacher and classroom context effects on student achievement: Implications for teacher evaluation. *Journal of Personnel Evaluation in Education,* 11, 57–67.

Yen, W.M. (1986). The choice of scale for educational measurement: An IRT perspective. *Journal of Educational Measurement,* 23, 299–326.

Yen, W.M. (1988). Normative growth expectations must be realistic: A reply to Phillips and Clarizio. *Educational Measurement: Issues and Practice,* 7(4), 16–17.

Yen, W.M. & Burket, G.R. (1997). Comparison of Item Response Theory and Thurstone methods of vertical scaling. *Journal of Educational Measurement,* 34(4), 293–313.